Advance Praise for *Sales T*

"*Sales Through the Eyes of a Climber* is real, drawing from the author's personal sales story and finding interesting and relevant parallels between sales and climbing, keeping the reader interested and engaged from cover to cover. With an appropriate and refreshing focus on success through win/win customer value creation, this book is one that I would recommend to anyone looking for a long-term career in sales, and especially those new to the profession."

—Brock Gavin, President
Arrow Truck Sales

"A great read that takes you on a personal journey of challenges of life, climbing and sales. Seth has a unique way of sharing his personal experiences with the reader and bringing out principles that are practical that can be applied! I would highly recommend this book not only to those in sales but to all that enjoys being on life's journey!"

—Paul Stephens, Vice President of Purchasing
Arrow Truck Sales

"To know Seth, is to know of his humility, his sincerity, and absolute passion for the success of others. Seth wrote this for our success, not the recognition of his own. This book pulled me in to where I felt I was on the rock wall, or in the office with him successfully growing sales. While reading, consider the journey you're on, stop, think, and listen to the encouragement – you will not be disappointed. To your success!"

—Jeff Oldham, CEO
GreenMark Equipment

STORY SCRIBE BOOKS

Kansas City   St. Louis

A division of The Story Scribe
www.thestoryscribe.com
816-377-8694

Cover and layout design by Kelly Ludden Design, LLC
www.kellyluddendesign.com

ISBN: 978-1-7327689-8-7
E-book ISBN: 978-1-7327689-9-4

Library of Congress Control Number: 2022935349

DISCLAIMER: The advice and suggestions presented in this book are based solely on the author's personal experience and not on scientific studies or statistical analyses. The methodology outlined in the book was developed through the highly subjective experiences of the author, and results may vary for readers.

Sales Through the Eyes of a Climber

*What Rock Climbing Taught Me
About the Art and Science of Sales*

BY

SETH PENN

STORY SCRIBE BOOKS

Kansas City   St. Louis

Dedication

To my forever girl, Desirea Penn. Without you, there wouldn't be a story, because I wouldn't have made it to where I am today.

Acknowledgment

There are many I'd like to thank for helping me get to where I am and for giving me a story worth telling.

To Trenton Pinckard, for recommending that I write a book because you would actually read it. (I did my part—your turn.)

A big thanks to Amy Woods Butler, my editor/coach, for pushing me and passionately teaching me how to write.

To Steve, for putting your neck out for me to get a job, for your friendship, and for your unwavering dedication to the best team in college football. (Go, Dawgs!)

To Paul, who not only hired me, but who is a major part of the person I am today.

To my mentor, Jim: You have no idea how much I respect you— despite you being a Bama fan. Your true kindness and patience are rare. Thank you for investing in me.

To Jason, who was bold and brave enough to ask what needed to be asked and for hanging with me long enough to get the answers. You aren't just good at throwing epic Halloween parties; you're pretty good at getting a lot out of your people, too.

To Chris, my best friend for life, and to Ian, Shannon, Michael, and Justin. We sure did have some fun.

Most of all, to my family. My parents, who guided me and patiently waited for me to grow up. To my wife and children, you can never fathom how important you all are to me. By reading this, I hope you all see clearly what is true. I love you all so much. From our little adventures to our big changes, I couldn't imagine a stronger family. So lucky.

And to the universe that dished up all the pain and failure I've struggled through—without those experiences, this story wouldn't be worth telling.

While I am undeserving of his grace, I thank God for loving me enough to allow growth. This story alone is proof enough that you have never abandoned me but rather have walked shoulder to shoulder with me, whether I wanted your presence or not. Thank you. I give you credit for any good in me.

Lastly, an acknowledgment for the woman who made this book possible. Writing it took me down an unusual path, one far more personal than I ever intended. The jog down memory lane reminded me why I am still so in love with my wife, Desirea. DZ, you are so amazing. I am so undeserving of you.

Table of Contents

Table of Contents

A Note from the Author

In the pages that follow, I describe my unusual journey to learning sales. Why unusual? Because several years of trial and error took place not just in front of customers, but on the face of vertical rock walls. It was largely while climbing that I began to see things in a new way, with fresh ideas that applied equally to life on the rock as they did on the ground, in front of customers.

The process wasn't short, and it wasn't easy. Over time I developed as a climber and as a salesperson—both due to paying attention, letting go of old ways, and considering things in a new light. Once I began applying to sales what I learned while climbing, I evolved from being a "three-trucks-a-month salesman" to consistently ranking among the top performers at the national truck dealership I work for. Within two years of being promoted to branch sales manager, my sales team and I turned a failing branch into a profitable one—proof that the concepts I developed could be learned and utilized by others.

Today, I work at the same company, now as Director of Training and Development. While writing this book in 2021, we had our best year in company history; more importantly, our customer satisfaction is as high as it has ever been. Love that! I'm incredibly honored that colleagues and team members have found success by applying these concepts. I hope you will too.

Prologue

I will never forget the morning that changed everything. I was driving to a vacant property in north Georgia to fill out yet another useless report that no one would ever read. The sun was just rising above the southern tip of the Blue Ridge Mountains, and the valley fog was beginning to lift. Between the rays from the sun above and the fog lifting from the ground below, my attention was drawn to a gray and white rock face looming above the valley. Just moments before, it had been nothing more than a dark shadow in the still of the morning. Now, with the sun in motion, the shadow had given way to the most spectacular burst of vibrant colors. I pulled over to the side of the road to check it out firsthand.

Full transparency: I nearly died that morning in my attempt to hike up to the base of the cliff. Not that it was a particularly difficult hike. It wasn't. No, what nearly killed me was how my effort to scrabble up the incline threw my out-of-shape, overweight body into wheezing, shuddering overdrive. I had to stop every few minutes to grab a pine sapling and catch my breath. Nothing unexpected there, but I hated that my focus was on survival instead of being present in the moment.

The hillsides were blanketed with clusters of green Georgia pines and piles of boulders fifteen, twenty, even thirty feet tall. The higher elevation gave the air a crisp, clean chill that motivated me to continue, despite getting more winded with each step I took. Aside from the sound of the occasional mountain spring or a bird chirping, the morning was still and quiet. It was a hard, upward fight as

I wove back and forth along the trail toward the base of rock face. Soon, the landscape started to open up. The trees and brush parted, and sunlight turned the leaves a new shade of brilliant green. That's when I saw it—the most beautiful thing I had ever laid eyes on. Reader, if you've ever gazed up at an enormous, never-ending chunk of rock, you understand my awe. The rock face in front of me was so impressive, so powerful, and so captivating that without a thought, overwhelmed and ignorant of where I was or even what I was doing, I grabbed a hold on the rock and started moving upward.

If you're thinking I was in over my head, you're right. I was wearing a pair of old tennis shoes and had absolutely no safety gear. The angle of the cliff wasn't too bad, but it was at least a hundred feet tall. That gave me plenty of time to ask myself, *What the hell are you doing, Seth?* But it didn't matter—my fear was dwarfed by the sheer joy of being on the rock. With every foot I ascended, I felt more alive and awake than I had in years.

I don't know exactly why it felt so incredible. Yes, it was a gorgeous morning, and I was surrounded by the beauty of Georgia hill country. I was exerting my body in ways I hadn't since I was a kid. And the sense of accomplishment when I reached the top of the cliff was something I'll never forget. But it was more than all that. For the first time in a long time—possibly ever—I had made a decision entirely for myself, without once considering what others would think of it. I am still so grateful that I didn't call my wife or my mom to tell them I was about to climb up the face of a cliff. I can only guess that if I had, I would have climbed right back into my truck and continued on to the vacant property to complete my meaningless report.

I fell in love with climbing that day, a love that would consume me for more than a decade. *So what?* you might be thinking. *What does that have to do with sales?*

In the upcoming pages, I share with you how climbing became a catalyst to a new way of viewing sales. The decision to pull off the road and climb that rock so long ago became the first step toward learning the concepts and core principles that I present to you here. It wasn't easy, and in most respects, the ever-more challenging climbs I undertook weren't even the hardest parts. The path to where I am today has been riddled with switchbacks, and there have been some massive falls along the way. But in the end, it's been more than worth it. I only hope that by writing about it, I can lead you along your own route up the cliff to sales success.

ONE

The Starting Point

"DADDY, DADDY!" I HEARD as I turned the knob of the front door after another long day of work. I had just finished cleaning up another abandoned home on the eastside of Atlanta. Ooh, what a dirty job: I worked for a contractor who did evictions. You know those boarded up houses covered with graffiti and surrounded by overgrown lawns? Yeah, that. The broken windows and dilapidated porches look pretty bad from the outside, but trust me, once you step in, it's way worse. Rotten food, soiled carpets, walls riddled with holes—and the smell! It's a stench that will burn the nose hairs. Needless to say, when I get home, I am a different kind of filthy.

When I stepped through the door, my two girls didn't care how gross I was. At one and two, they were small enough to wrap their little bodies around my legs and plop their butts on top of my feet. They giggled with every step I took towards the kitchen (which, in our tiny home, wasn't very many). Desirea was pulling the chicken from the oven when she turned to smile at me. A petite five foot two with porcelain skin and blonde hair, she was by far the most beautiful part of my day. Even after several years of being together, I couldn't believe my luck; I had outkicked my coverage with her by a mile.

"How was your day?" she asked.

"The usual, busy but good."

As she stirred the mac and cheese, she turned my way again with eyebrows raised. "Did you actually have the tools to do the job right this time?"

My girls tightened their grip as I gave each of them a little shake. Their giggles became happy screeches, and I had to answer a little louder to combat the noise. "He had me use screws instead of bolts for the windows. Oh, and the mower cut off again."

I didn't mind my job, I really didn't. What I did mind was how I never had the equipment or supplies to do it right. The guy I worked for, Delmar, made tons of money as a subcontractor for a bigger company, but he found a way to spend every last dime of it, and then some, without investing any of the profits back into the business. We were chronically short on the supplies we needed; even worse, he'd recently stopped paying me on time—or sometimes paying me at all. "I'll square up with you next week," he would say. And he did—just often enough to keep me from quitting.

Desirea gave me a sympathetic look. She would be the one dealing with the collection calls again when things got bad, but nevertheless, she always empathized with me. Boy, I had hit the jackpot with her. What a supportive wife... and cook! After she placed the forks on the table, she leaned down to eye level with our girls to tell them that dinner was ready. They released their grip on my legs and scrambled to the table.

"I'm sure ready!" I said. I was starved. The girls climbed up in their chairs, and I was about to follow when Desirea threw her arm in front of my chest.

"You're going to take a shower first, right?"

The thought of leaving a steaming dinner had me mildly annoyed, but there wasn't a world that existed where DZ was going to allow me to get away with coming to the table looking—and smelling—like I did. I remember wanting a wife with a backbone. I got it, and hers happened to be constructed out of titanium. "Yes, dear." In four steps, I had reached the hall closet to grab a towel and in another five, I was in the bathroom. Did I mention our house was small? I figured struggling was just a normal thing for a young family like us.

The next week at work, I was carrying a moldy nightstand from a vacant property when my phone rang.

"Seth?"

I threw the nightstand into the trailer. "Yes, this is him," I said distractedly as I wiped the mold and dust from my hands.

"This is Mr. Haney."

I froze. Mr. Haney was the president of the company my boss was contracted to do jobs for. *Oh, god*, I thought. He must have spot-checked the property I'd told Desirea about. "Yes sir, if you're calling about the property off Highway 278, I can explain about the screws on the window—"

"I don't know anything about that, but Seth, listen. I need to ask you a question."

My head spun. What could this be about, I wondered.

A moment later, he said, "I'm done with Delmar. He hasn't been running things well for some time. I'm letting him go. My question for you is, do you want to take his spot?"

I scrambled to wrap my mind around what he just asked. *What a great opportunity! Take over my own operation!* But as soon as I thought it, doubts rushed in. How could I possibly do it? Financially, there was no way. As a contractor, I would be responsible for acquiring all the supplies, tools, and vehicles. Shaking my head and desperately wanting more time to piece this loaded question together, I responded the only way I could. "I'm so sorry sir, I can't."

He must have seen this coming. "Is this because of money?"

My ego sank. "Yes, sir." Without realizing it, I'd been pacing back and forth beside the truck. The other guy on my work crew gave me a quizzical look as he dumped a commode into the back of the trailer. "I don't have the money to buy into it," I said.

Mr. Haney let out a slow breath. "How about this, Seth. I'll provide you with a truck, a trailer, and a sizable loan to start out."

My dirty fingers squeezed against my temples as I attempted to take in the conversation. Did I have the courage to take this on? "When would you want me to do this?"

I could hear his smile as he replied. "Immediately."

That call changed my life. It was a whirlwind, really—I went from wondering if a bank card was going to get declined at a restaurant to being able to walk into a Pier 1 without throwing up. Our financial struggles appeared to be over. Desirea had been working part-time as a bartender (the hottest one in the place), but soon after we got up and running, she happily made the transition to being a full-time mom. The next few years were great. In no time, we had acquired three trucks and several trailers for the business. We moved out of our small starter home to a new Craftsman-style home outside of the city, and for the first time in our life together, there was no shortage of vacations, toys for our girls, and new cars for us.

Our new neighborhood had plenty of younger couples like us. We'd been there about a week when I heard, "What's up, neighbor!"

I'd been carrying a tote from my truck to the garage. Somewhat startled, I turned to see a tall guy about my age wearing a Georgia Bulldogs hat standing nearby in the grass. Immediately, I dropped the tote and extended a hand. "I'm Seth."

He shook my hand with a smile. "I'm Steve. Nice to have you next door."

Desirea must have heard us talking from the garage, and with a curious smile, she walked out into the driveway.

"This is my wife, Desirea, and we have two little ones running around somewhere."

Steve turned back toward his house and called for his wife. When she appeared out of their garage, two sets of eyeballs peered around the corner behind her.

"You have little ones too, huh?" I said, waving in the direction of their half-hidden faces.

"We do. And this is my wife, Andrea."

I sensed immediately we were going to be friends, and I was right. From that point on, it wasn't uncommon to see us at each other's houses. From backyard barbecues to helping each other with home projects, Steve and I were almost inseparable. That was true for our wives and kids as well. There were no property lines as far as the kids were concerned, and honestly, we didn't mind at all. Whether it was playing cards, hosting parties, or enjoying a few cold ones on Saturdays watching football, life was good. There wasn't a morning I woke up without thinking how lucky I was. Hot wife, beautiful girls, my own company, a big house, good friends, nice vehicles, and I was getting stronger and stronger as a climber.

Oh, yeah, back to climbing...I was freaking all in! I spent every night in the gym and even taped pictures of people climbing in front of the weight bench just to keep myself motivated. My weight was dropping, my muscles were getting stronger, and I was doing climbs that were progressively more vertical. I had moved beyond counting calories and gym time; I was now living for my new pastime. I woke up every morning, checked the weather to see if rain was in the forecast, and if it was clear, I was quick to rearrange my day so I could climb between jobs. I built a rock wall inside our house and climbed it daily. I dressed differently, spent money differently, and conversed differently—climbing became everything I talked about (apologies to all my family and friends for that, by the way). Yep, from Walmart to REI, shops with climbing gear became my toy stores, and I cruised through the climbing section of their websites regularly. "Hey, Seth, here is REI's new magazine. See anything in there you want?" What a crazy question for my wife to ask. "Heck yeah, I do!" Just the mention of new stuff and I was in the car, heading over to see the gear in person. REI had everything from climbing shoes to harnesses, ropes and all of the items needed for safety. Also alpine draws (carabiners with webbing) and cams (protection that expands to fit in cracks on the wall). And since I also enjoyed bouldering, I never left without eyeing the back wall that stocked their selection of crash pads (basically a glorified mattress). At checkout, I grabbed the newest climbing magazine. Never would miss that!

My obsession was driven by the desire to climb the hardest, most impossible-looking route, which before long meant climbing upside down. I'm not going to lie, hearing a passing stranger say, "Oh, my god, that is insane! I would never!" felt pretty good to my ego, but mostly I enjoyed the serenity of being outside, testing myself to the limit. It wasn't just the physical aspect but also the mental challenge that made my new hobby so addictive—facing the fear. Every time I freaked out but pushed ahead in spite of my emotions, the joy that followed was euphoric; it became a drug, and an addictive one at that. "OH, YES!" I'd yell, as my right hand would slam and clinch to a hold that hadn't looked possible from hundreds of feet below. Oh, those moments....Today, I could close a bar down telling stories of being scared out of my mind high up on a wall. I lived for that crap.

The more interested in climbing I became, the less interested I became in my work. But while the jobs themselves weren't as exciting as they used to be, the lifestyle they afforded Desirea and me never lost its luster. So what if I had to clean maggot-infested food out of a refrigerator that hadn't seen electricity in months? After a dry heave or two, I would just remind myself that cleaning it paid hundreds. *Money,* Seth, *really good money!* That's all I needed to remind myself to continue. Splat! Another rotten and rancid piece would hit the trash.

In early 2008, I woke to the usual sound of my 4:30 a.m. alarm. Half asleep, I made my way to the kitchen to start a pot of coffee, then climbed the stairs to my office to print the jobs for the day.

"Anything good come in?" I heard from the kitchen before my feet even made it to the computer. I hadn't heard Desirea get up. Not that her wakefulness was a complete shock. Neither of us had been sleeping well. In the past several weeks, the flow of incoming work had diminished greatly; aside from being confused, we were both starting to get concerned.

"Just two bids," I answered. I clicked "print" on the computer. I was paid only twenty-five dollars per bid, and judging by the location of these two, I'd be spending more than that on gas. Rounding the corner at the bottom of the steps, I saw Desirea standing with both palms pressed on our granite countertop. "So much for having all our eggs in one basket," she said. "This is getting rough."

I nodded. My business was a hundred percent dependent on government-backed loans, and until recently, that had translated into job security. But the housing market was in trouble, and that trouble was trickling down to us. *It's bound to get better soon,* I thought.

I was wrong. Over the next few weeks, things grew steadily worse.

"HEY!!!" I heard Desirea shout one morning as I was shaving. I startled and nearly cut myself.

Desirea yelled down from the office. "Seth, you got a really good job!"

I threw the razor down and flew up the stairs to see for myself. As I bounded into the office, she handed me the paper she'd just printed off. "I knew it would turn around, Seth!" she said, a huge smile lighting up her face.

I looked at the sheet of paper and then slowly dropped it onto the desk. It wasn't a job at all, just another lousy twenty-five-dollar bid. My head dropped. My beautiful wife slowly shut her eyes, her hope shattered. "It isn't a good job, is it?" I slowly shook my head as I raised my eyes to look at her. "This isn't going to get better, is it?" she asked.

"No, DZ, I don't think it will."

At first, we had assumed the derailment would be temporary, but as the days passed, things continued to look worse. I wanted to ignore it, to pretend that it'd get better soon, but with mounting bills and almost no income, it was time to face reality. After the girls left for school, I poured Desirea and myself some more coffee. "I need to call Mr. Haney's office to get some answers. We have to know if it's going to continue like this, or if we just need to wait it out."

She nodded, gave me a kiss, and walked into our bedroom to give me some privacy. With my stomach in my throat, I dialed the phone. Mr. Haney's office manager picked up.

"Morning," I said. "I really hate to call about this, but it sure feels like I haven't gotten any work lately. Is everything okay?"

Silence. After a moment, I heard the manager sigh. "Sorry, Seth, but we don't see an end to this. The housing market is a mess, and it's going to get even worse. We just don't have any work for our subcontractors. I can't say much more. Take care of yourself, Seth."

I dropped the phone to my side and stared out the back window. That had to be the most concerning group of words I had ever heard. If my contractor was losing hope about getting any work, I didn't stand a chance.

In a daze, I placed the phone on the granite counter and looked around. The girls had left a pile of toys in the middle of the kitchen floor, next to the pricey dining set we'd bought just the year before. On the counter, a fancy new coffee machine, my birthday gift to Desirea, was gurgling. *We're going to lose it all*, I thought, burying my face in my palms.

A few minutes later, Desirea walked around the corner. "What did they say, hon?" she asked softly.

I gave a quick laugh—I knew she'd been on the other side of that wall with her ear against it. But she had been patient, and honestly, she deserved to know the whole story. I did my best to replay what had been said, but once the first few words came out, so did the tears—from both of us. With all of our personal and business loans, we were almost a million dollars in debt. Our days of living in comfort were over.

Spring turned into summer. A few jobs trickled in, but there wasn't a day without stress as we struggled to stay afloat. Oh, how I missed being carefree and happy! One day as I was peering through the back window, watching a few leaves drop from the trees, I had a thought.

"Hey, DZ," I said, "instead of sulking at home again this weekend, why don't we go out west for a vacation?"

"Dude, Seth," she said with a downbeat tone. "What part of 'we're broke' do you not understand? No!"

But my mind was already racing ahead, imagining the climbs I could do near Las Vegas. Yes, we were going broke and our situation seemed hopeless, and climbing was still on my mind all the time.

Desirea started walking away, but I thought fast. "We can go with Jenny and Micah! It will be good for us."

She grabbed a bath towel as she continued toward the hamper. I was now begging, and she was having none of it.

"I can't believe you would even think about climbing right now."

I reached out to grab her hand. With her eyes closed and with a heavy sigh, she spoke. "What, Seth?"

In my most loving, sympathetic, sincere voice, I said, "It's just that we've both been under a lot of stress. You deserve some time away with Jenny." Desirea rolled her eyes and gave a small laugh. She knew I was full of crap, but she reluctantly agreed anyway. Before she had a chance to change her mind, I booked the plane tickets and the room. We were going!

Once we landed in Vegas, I saw that the pictures I had pored over for years didn't begin to do it justice. This place was awesome. You could spend a lifetime climbing here and never run out of amazing routes, climbs on stone that transitioned not only in color, but in style as well. "Isn't this beautiful, girl?" I said, pointing out the window of the rental car. My wife had never been to Vegas either, and the landscape was having the same effect on her.

"It really is," she whispered.

Behind the canyons, snow-capped mountains drew a jagged line across the sky. Seeing snow in early fall was quite the contrast to our usual experience. Every direction we looked took our breath away.

That weekend we had a blast hiking, climbing, and exploring with our friends. The three days came and went too quickly, and before we knew it, we found ourselves waiting in the terminal for our return flight. It had made sense when I booked the trip to spend what little money we had on a good, albeit short, vacation, but once the wheels of our plane touched ground in Atlanta, regret set in. What had I been thinking? We shouldn't have done this.

We piled into Micah and Jenny's car for the ride home from the airport, and as we turned the corner to our street, I glanced up at our house. "Oh, god," I murmured under my breath. Desirea saw what I did, and we whipped our heads to face each other in a mild panic. Our house was completely dark.

"Oh man, the power must be out," I said, although I knew better. I thought of the large stack of mail, some of which had red lettering on it, that I had stopped opening weeks ago.

"Perhaps someone hit a line," Desirea blurted out.

Our neighbors' houses were lit up like it was Christmas.

Micah and Jenny remained silent, for which I was grateful. "Well, thanks for the ride," I said. I quickly grabbed our suitcases, and Desirea and I gave them a wave as they drove off. "Nothing to see here," our wave said. "Just a couple of friends who haven't paid their electric bill!"

"Good times!" I said, as we turned to walk toward our light-deprived home. Once inside, I flipped a switch just to see if something would happen. Nothing did. Quietly, Desirea opened the fridge and without a word began to throw out all the rotten food, while I started making calls in an attempt to get the power turned back on (it didn't work). Desirea lit some candles, and we called to check in with the kids at their grandparents' house. An hour later, DZ was getting ready for bed when I heard, "The water is off, too?!?"

Sleep didn't come easy for us, and after a long, restless night, Desirea got out of bed first. I thought she was making coffee, but that would have required power (which we did not have) and water (which we also did not have). *How in the hell did we get here*, I thought. I threw the sheets to the side and made my way to the kitchen. Desirea was sitting hunched in a chair at the breakfast table, rolling her engagement ring between her fingers with tears in her eyes. She looked my way, gave half a smile, and dropped the ring onto the table.

"No, Desirea, we don't need to do this," I protested.

She looked at me and slowly nodded. Her lips read, "We do," but her vocal cords forgot to do their part. I quietly sat in the chair beside her. After a few moments of silence, she stood up and left the room, leaving her ring on the table. I sat there by myself for an hour, then drove to the pawn shop, ring in hand.

Two months had passed since I had pawned Desirea's ring, and while that money had been enough to get the utilities back on, there was nothing left over. Talk about a sinking ship! On this day I had a job in Atlanta—yes, you read that right, reader, one single job. I'd gone from having up to twenty jobs on a given day to just one. On the upside, at least I'd be getting home early.

When I finished at the property, I gave Desirea a call to let her know I'd be home soon. With an uptick in tone, she responded with, "Great! I'll make dinner!"

As soon as we hung up, my phone rang. "Hey Seth, any chance I can borrow your crash pad?" It was my friend Rob, calling from a climbing area. I smiled at his question. He knew I always had my climbing stuff with me.

"Of course, dude! Where you at?" I heard the sound of Rob clapping his hands in celebration.

"Awesome, bud. I'm just outside of Atlanta."

Ten minutes later, I was pulling into a gravel lot. Knowing I would be dropping off the gear and would be back on the road in a few minutes, I hadn't bothered to mention the little detour to my wife. No climbing for me.

I grabbed the gear and began hiking down the trail to where Rob was sitting by a little boulder. With a wide smile and motioning with chalk-covered hands, he went on and on about the new project (in case you're not a climber, a "project" is a new route that you haven't climbed yet).

"I've never seen this climbed, and I'm starting to understand why," Rob said. "Crazy hard but cool!"

Looking the rock up and down, I nodded in agreement. The ground was covered in roots and small divots. "I can see why you need the pad," I said.

"Want to try it out since you're here?"

I held up my climbing shoes with a grin. So maybe I did intend to do some climbing. I was ecstatic at the chance to forget about my work troubles for a few minutes. "But I have to make it quick. I'm not really supposed to be here," I said.

The next twenty minutes were a blast, but I knew Desirea was gonna kill me if I made it home any later. Switching back into my street shoes, I said goodbye to Rob, then hurried off. Running up the wooded trail back to the parking lot, my mind was in daydream mode—climbing was still my drug, inducing just as much euphoria as it ever had. Suddenly, as I rounded the last curve in the trail, my attention snapped into focus. I did a 360, then did it again...."Didn't I park here?" I was confused. Maybe my eyes were playing tricks on me. "I did. I did park here," I said out loud. My eyes panned the small gravel lot. The small—and, except for Rob's car, vacant—lot.

Gone. Everything was gone. No truck, no trailer, nothing. Several minutes passed while I stood in disbelief before the realization fully sank in. I'd been robbed! I grabbed my phone out of my shorts, but I didn't make a call; I just stared at it. Was I hoping the thieves might bring it all back? No, this wasn't optimism, it was fear. With a deep breath, I finally dialed.

"Hey, sweetheart," I said.

"Hi, dear." Desirea seemed more resigned than surprised by my call. I could tell she knew this wasn't going to be good news. My stomach had already dropped, but now my heart followed suit.

I had barely explained what happened when she stopped me short. "I'll get the girls together and come as quick as I can." I slid my phone back into my pocket and sat down on a rock that served as the border between the gravel and woods. Currently, it would serve as purgatory.

Forty-five mind-numbing minutes later, I watched her car emerge on the gravel road, and the sick feeling in my stomach intensified. I faked a smile as my girls waved out the back windows. Oh, the joy of being a child; they had no idea. My smile disappeared when I jumped into the front seat next to Desirea. Her look said it all: I had better start talking, fast. I'm never afraid of anything Desirea says, but her silence strikes a fear like no other. She stared straight ahead as I rambled on and on. As we waited for the police to arrive, I kept talking, and Desirea never said a word. Ten minutes passed, then twenty. I kept glancing her way, but she refused to return the favor. I didn't know what to do. Finally, the girls started to chatter about their day, and while I was grateful that they were filling the silence, I barely took in what they were saying. My thoughts were in another place. This was hell.

Another ten minutes went by before I saw the police cruiser pull up. "Finally!" I shouted. The officer took down the information, but she told me straightaway that there was little chance my truck or any of its contents would ever be recovered.

TWO

The Aftermath

"**W**E HAVE TO CLOSE the business," I said in a slow, somber voice as I flung the keys on the counter. Our forty-five-minute car ride had been mostly quiet aside from the occasional laughter from one of our girls, but now that we were home, we needed to have this conversation in full. With no truck, no tools, and no equipment, I had no way of completing any jobs. My business was officially dead.

My first comment didn't get a response from DZ, so I tried again. "Insurance money isn't going to scratch the surface of what we need," I said, stealing a glance her way. Still nothing. She walked towards the kitchen to turn the oven back on in silence. Then she exhaled audibly.

"I guess we don't really have a choice." Cabinet doors were opened and closed repeatedly and pots, plates, and skillets appeared on the counter. My beautiful wife was deflecting.

"Hey!" I said in a direct tone to get her attention. "Are we really doing this?"

Just then, something behind me moved, and as I turned, two shadows darted off to a bedroom. Desirea gave me The Look. No more discussion while the girls were still awake.

For so long, we had hidden our mounting troubles from the girls, but the situation was getting the best of us, and we knew it. A few more moments passed before Desirea looked me straight in the eye. "Yeah, I guess we are." I could see tears welled up in her eyes, but before they fell, she had turned to face the stove, her back to me. "Seth, it's your turn today. Let me cook."

"My turn." That's what we'd been reduced to—taking turns walking down the driveway to the mailbox to collect all the envelopes marked "Final Notice." When Desirea used my first name, I knew not to argue.

"Okay, girlie," I said, feigning a bravery I didn't feel. At the mailbox, I gave a deep, long sigh as I pulled out the latest batch of overdue bills. Would this ever end?

The next Monday morning, I received a call from the police. "We found your truck."

They'd found it! Maybe everything would go back to normal after all. "Great! Where is it?" For three brief seconds, there was complete silence.

"In a swamp."

"In a swamp?"

The officer cleared his throat before confirming. "Yes, we found it partially submerged in a swamp."

A short while later, with the kids in the back of the car, DZ and I stood at the location the officer had given me. There was no missing it. My truck stood nose-down in the swamp. A tow truck pulled it out, but the damage had been done. Total loss.

Over the next few months, we spent our days jumping from one catastrophe to the next. Opening the mailbox had been the most gut-wrenching part of the day, but now that we were expecting a check from the auto insurance company, it was the only hopeful moment of the day. I don't know if you can relate, reader, but the emotional rollercoaster of experiencing hope and total despair within seconds is staggering. When the check finally came, we paid the "red letter" bills and stashed what was left over. That was the last income we would see for a long time.

With our world in chaos, I was still running to the one thing that would make me feel great about myself: climbing. There I'd be, sitting on my couch, my mind churning away on how I could fix things, when suddenly the phone would ring.

"Hey brother, you up for climbing this weekend?" one of my buddies would ask.

I never hesitated. "Hell, yeah!" Only after agreeing to go climb, I'd turn away from the phone to yell, "Desirea, is it cool if I go climbing this weekend?"

"I guess so."

She never said no. No matter how often I wanted to go—and by this point, it was the only thing I wanted to do, the only relief from my financial worries—Desirea always said the same thing: "I guess so." Climbing was my escape, but mine alone. Yes, while my wonderful wife sat at home with the girls, not knowing if and when the money would come in, I went out to play. The only thing my family had was us, and I took the "us" away by running away to climb.

One rainy day I was at the climbing gym when I met a cool couple, Justin and Jessica. They'd been climbing for quite some time, but always at the gym; they had never tried climbing outdoors. "When do you wanna go?" I asked.

Jessica turned toward Justin before answering. "This Friday would work—we're clear the whole weekend!"

I was so excited that as soon as I got home, I hurried into the garage to get setups for three: three harnesses, three chalk bags, thr—

"What are you doing?"

I jumped. Oh crap, I was so focused on the trip that I'd forgotten to tell Desirea I was home! "Hey DZ, I had a great time today!" I quickly told her about meeting Justin and Jessica and our plans for the overnight trip.

She was slow to respond. "And that's this weekend?" she asked. "Are you sure?"

I couldn't help but notice her puzzled look. "Yep!" I confirmed with a happy grin. She nodded and turned to walk back inside. I resumed counting to three.

That Friday afternoon, I picked up my new friends and by evening, we were enjoying a fire at our campsite in Alabama. The next day, we did a full day of climbing, with me in the lead, which on this beginner-level climb, didn't come with much risk. Both of them acclimated. Success! Sunday morning, I led a tall but easier route for them to climb laps on. This particular route stood higher than the rest, and the vantage point gave a panoramic view of the world below. I had a thought: *How cool would it be to call Desirea from the top?* I grabbed my phone from my pocket and dialed her number.

"Hey, you!" I said. "Just wanted to tell you how much I love you and I hope you're having a great day!"

"Oh, hi, Seth." Her tone told me that no, she wasn't having a great day.

"What are you up to?" I asked.

"We're going to see my mom and then afterward I'll probably run the girls over to see my grandma."

"That's a lot of travel in one day. Why are you going both places?"

Hey, reader, you ready for this? (I sure wasn't.)

"It seems like the right thing to do on Mother's Day," she replied.

OH, MY GOD! What a jackass I was! The mother of my children and on Mother's Day, the one day that's supposed to be all about her, I call her from the top of a freaking rock hundreds of miles away. How could I be so stupid?

There is no recovering from something like that, and back at home, there was no recovering from what was happening to us. Our days turned into weeks, and weeks turned into months. We learned that the only thing more stressful than opening a "Final Notice" letter is when they stop coming. Date nights had long been a thing of the past; now we spent our evenings peering through the blinds for the repo guy. And while we were only one payment behind on our utilities, the mortgage was a different story.

One morning, my wife came up to me with tears in her eyes, and she buried her head in my chest. "What are we going to do?" I assumed that the stress was really getting to her, so I gave her a hug in an attempt to comfort her. That's when I noticed she was holding something in her hand. Desirea backed away from my chest to look at me. I glanced down and my stomach sank. It was a pregnancy test. A positive pregnancy test.

Oh, poor girl...Can you even imagine? Slowly, we slid our backs down our bedroom wall until our butts hit the carpet. It's not that we didn't want another child, but now? When we were flat broke with no end in sight? Hours passed with nothing more than the sound of Desirea's sniffles until, at last, she broke the silence. "The timing couldn't be worse! What are we going to do? How are we going to survive?" There was nothing I could say to alleviate the desperation we were experiencing. Nothing I could say to make things better.

The next day, the girls left for school, and I sat down to sip my coffee. Outside, I heard laughter. Not the "Ha ha, that's funny!" kind of laughter, more the "somebody-is-losing-it" crazy kind. The door busted open, and in walked my wife. "You just can't make this up!" In her hand was a piece of paper that had been stuck to our front door. From the bank. They wanted their house back.

After all those years of cleaning up houses in foreclosure, the irony of it happening to us hit me hard. There was nothing funny about it, but I laughed. Like Desirea's, it sounded like the haw-haws of a crazy person on the brink. "Guess we need to have a garage sale," I said sarcastically.

With a wry smile and without missing a beat, Desirea responded. "No, we need to have a 'we-need-to-sell-every-freaking-thing-we-own-because-we-need-money' sale." She continued, "You know, I knew that this was going to be painful, but I really didn't expect this to carry on for so long. It's like our life is a TV series!"

"Ha! We are a TV series!" I said, my laughter sounding downright psychotic. I stood up to meet the girl of my dreams eye level as we continued to laugh. I wrapped my arms around her waist, and we smiled at each other. Laughter is good for the soul, and just listening to my wife be sarcastic made me happier about our crappy situation. I think we both recognized this as a defining moment; it was time to take ownership of our situation, together.

Early that Saturday morning, Desirea was in delegation mode. "Let's get these out before daylight," she said, pointing to the signs we'd made the night before announcing the garage/ "everything" sale. "While you're doing that, the girls and I will pull the tables out into the drive and set everything up."

When I returned, cars were already beginning to fill the street with buyers hungry for what remained of our previously comfortable existence. Throughout the day, I watched my wife close her eyes in pain as one keepsake or toy after another got carried off by a stranger. We accepted low-ball offers on our high-end appliances, and I watched helplessly as all of the remaining equipment and tools that had been vital to my business were purchased for pennies on the dollar. Our entire day was spent shaking our heads in disbelief. At four that afternoon, a guy reversed his trailer into our drive and loaded up the washer, dryer, and extra fridge. By day's end, our house had the kind of emptiness that makes a voice echo. Devastating, simply devastating. I would've never predicted that we'd be in this situation; never predicted that we'd be sitting front and center as our entire world burned to the ground.

The next day, I saw our neighbor Steve in his driveway. He'd been at home the day before, but not once had he walked outside, which was unusual.

"Hey, Steve," I said.

He must have had an idea of what was happening with us, but he and I had never discussed it. I could tell he was embarrassed. "So," he said, "Things have changed quite a bit lately, huh?"

That was all I needed. The horrors of the past months gushed out of me, about the truck and the bills and selling off our belongings just to survive. Telling him was therapeutic. I spilled everything; at the end there was nothing more to hide. Then, the conversation took a turn.

With eyes cast downward and one foot distractedly skimming over a patch of grass, Steve said, "You know, I could put in a good word for you at my company, if you like?" He worked in sales for a used truck dealership. His head lifted just enough to catch my gaze.

"Sure, Steve, if you think it might work," I said. Why did I feel I had to play it poker-faced? I was thrilled! "I'd appreciate that."

The next day, he talked to his boss and got the thumbs up. They were willing to consider me. I filled out an application that evening. That next Tuesday, I drove to the used truck lot for my interview with Paul, Steve's manager. From the moment I met him, he struck me as an optimist full of energy. Every question or statement that exited his mouth ended on an uptick of tone.

"Seth? Great. Great to see you. Sit down, sit down," he said with a warm smile, gesturing toward a chair. Nervously, I took a seat. He shut the door on a small but bustling office and sat down across from me. We chatted for a few minutes, then, getting down to business, he asked, "Have you ever sold trucks before?" My mind raced. I hadn't sold semi-trucks but I had sold cars, Kirby vacuums, and even speakers out of a van. And, hey! Most recently, I was successful at selling everything I owned, so there was that…

"Uh, no sir, but I have sold before."

Paul's eyes lit up with interest. "Oh really, what have you sold?"

I gave him the list that had just run through my mind (omitting the part about selling most of our worldly possessions). Paul slapped his hands together and laughed; obviously, he was pleased and probably a little amused at the diversity of my experience. He asked a few more questions, then sent me to fill out paperwork and take a drug test. I had the job.

Desirea was excited when I told her the news on the way back home. While we knew that there was no chance to match the income we'd had when I was a subcontractor, at least there was some relief in sight.

"What's up, brother? You wanna climb this weekend to celebrate my new job?" I said on the phone to my friend Chris. He was my second call after DZ. With my new employment settled, my mind had skittered back to its obsession.

"You got the job? That's awesome, dude. Heck yeah, I want to celebrate!"

Remember how I mentioned that I could close down a bar with all the stories I have of climbing and being freaked out on a wall? Most of those climbs took place with Chris. We'd been friends for years, and I'd always looked up to him. In typical climber fashion, he has a slim build, and with his reddish beard and wild hair, he looks the part of a mountain dude. He is loud and, just like Desirea, he never leaves his audience confused about where he stands on any subject. When you first meet him, he comes across as an energetic social butterfly, but the more you get to know him, the clearer it is that, like me, he just wants his small circle of people. Some say he's a butthole at times. I agree, he agrees, opinion noted. But he is loyal to a fault and would make the short list of people to call if I needed to hide a body. (I've never used that card, but just sayin'.)

"Where you heading?" he asked.

"North Carolina sounds like a fun time," I suggested, only half-jokingly.

Chris laughed. "You don't want to just climb. You want a big wall adventure! Right?" He had a knack for figuring me out.

"Yeah, something tall and scary sounds perfect to me!"

It takes more than physical ability to be a great climbing partner. When you're pushing up against your absolute physical limits, you have to trust that the person holding the other end of the rope will not let you down, and not just metaphorically. They literally hold your life in their hands. Throughout my and Chris's many adventures together, being physically tethered to each other with a rope had also bonded our spirits.

"How about heading up to Cashiers?" Chris asked. Cashiers was a small mountain town that served as the gateway to some giant walls.

"Perfect!"

On Friday, Chris picked me up early mid-afternoon, and the next four hours passed quickly. We reminisced about past adventures and planned what we were going to do the next day. Past the sleepy little town of Cashiers, the pavement turned to dirt, and a surge of joy shot through me. The sun was setting over the western mountain tops, casting long shadows mixed with yellow hues. As soon as we reached the parking area, we jumped out to take in the fresh mountain air.

"It's late, dude. Want to camp at the car tonight and start in early tomorrow?" Chris asked.

The only way to reach the base of the wall was a three-mile hike over meadows, across streams, and through some seriously dense undergrowth. Beyond that, a series of relentless and unforgiving switchbacks led the way down for six hundred feet to the bottom. It's a brutal approach.

"I say we hike in as far as we can tonight," I answered, grabbing my backpack.

"Let's do it."

After packing the rope, climbing gear, and the lightest camping supplies we had, we were off. Heaven. The place was absolutely beautiful, with thick laurels and views for miles. It's a shame that my mind had to fight between enjoying the scene and shifting into a sort of daydream mode. It's what I did before every gutsy climb, no exceptions: run through every detail in my mind about how I was going to do it. The visualization technique was what had gotten me so far so fast as a climber.

We pitched camp a few miles in, and before daylight the next morning, the water was boiling for coffee and our bags were packed. It was still dark as we started down the never-ending switchbacks, but soon the sun came up and started working its magic. Beams of light split through the foliage in explosions of color. As I was focused on tip-toeing past a washed-out section of the trail, I heard Chris yell from in front of me, "I freaking love this!" He stopped to look skyward. The massive rock stood over a thousand feet high, and I couldn't even begin to guess how wide.

"Me too, dude. Me too."

A few minutes later, we reached the start of the climb. I dropped my pack and began arranging my gear, and moments later, we were climbing. The first few hundred feet were fairly easy. The view above the canopy of trees was breathtaking as the sun burned away the clouds, and we could see for miles. I was inspired. "Onward!" I yelled out at the top of my lungs. I was feeling it. Off our belay ledge, a balance-y but doable stretch of stone stood before us. Chris, now below me, was feeling it, too.

"You got this!" he called up to me.

Onward and upward I climbed. For seventy-five feet it was smooth sailing, but just as soon as I let my guard down, POP! Before I could flinch, I was airborne. I slid and bounced hard off the rock as I plummeted, a terrifying descent that didn't stop until my rope pulled taut, and I slammed into the stone one final time.

"Oh, man," I moaned, as I clutched my side. Something was seriously wrong. Every time I took a breath, an intense pain radiated from my left rib cage. Holding my chest tight, I attempted to yell. "Chris!"

"Yeah dude, what happened? You okay?" I could hear his voice, but it sounded like it was above me. Oh my god, how far did I fall? The stabbing pain was growing stronger, but I drew the deepest breath I could to answer. "I think we need to go back down."

"Whatever you need, Seth." I could hear the concern in his voice.

We worked together for about thirty minutes until we were standing on the same ledge.

"Dude, what happened?" he asked.

Hunched over, head hanging, I attempted to remember. "I think a hold broke." With a worried look, Chris quickly set up the rope for our rappel. I was in agony.

Repelling down was uncomfortable, but that was nothing compared to the switchbacks on the hike back to the car. Before long, I was coughing up blood and stopping every few feet to catch my breath. "My ribs must be broken," I mumbled. Every inhale was hell. Slowly, step by step, we reached the parking lot. It had taken several hours, and now it was now dark. But it wasn't over yet; we still had a four-hour drive to get home. Why didn't I have Chris take me to the local hospital, you might be wondering? I'm a dude, that's why. I knew something was seriously wrong, but that didn't stop me from downplaying it to Chris.

We were both quiet in the car. Two hours into the drive, he turned to look at me. "You okay, man?"

He must have caught a grimace on my face. "Yup, I'm good. Probably just bruised a rib."

I was in tremendous pain, but the only thing I thought about was how disappointed Desirea would be. I reclined the seat and closed my eyes, but I couldn't fall asleep. I was supposed to start my new job in two days—two days! We were broke, had been for a long time, and now that I had a chance for an income, I had messed it up. I knew from the pain in my chest that I had done some serious damage to my lung. The same sickening feeling I'd had when I was robbed returned. I had messed up again, right when things were about to turn around for us.

"Feel better, brother," Chris said when he dropped me off at home.

"Sure, I'll feel fine in the morning," I said, hoping it would be true.

It wasn't. Getting out of bed the next morning was painful, and when Desirea handed me a coffee cup, I dropped it. In an instant, Desirea's normal, cheerful smile disappeared.

"What is going on? What did you do to yourself?"

I hadn't said anything when I returned the night before, still clinging to the hope that the pain would disappear on its own. I started to explain, but trying to speak made me double over in a fit of coughing.

Desirea stuck out her hand toward me. "Stop." I had no fight in me to argue. Throwing on a hoodie, she said, "You are such a boy, you know it? What am I gonna do with you?"

We all know that waiting in the lobby of the emergency room is no fun. But here's something you might not know: If you double over while coughing up blood, your wait time is a lot shorter. That being said, it isn't reassuring when they haul you in immediately before anyone else because your life could be on the line.

THREE

A Few Days of Hell

AFTER THE X-RAY, the doctors were quick to set an IV. Turns out, they needed me semi-unconscious so they could jam a quarter-inch tube between my ribs. (Thank freaking god for anesthetic!) My silent fears had been confirmed. Not only were my two bottom ribs broken, but my lung had collapsed, and they were using the tube to reinflate it. Unfortunately, they wanted to keep me several days for observation, so along with blowing my lung, I assumed I had blown my chance at the new job.

From the hospital bed, I dialed a few numbers. "Hey, Steve, you won't believe this…"

Then, "Hey, Chris, you won't believe this…"

Then, "Hey, Mom…"

Well, you get the point. But the call I was avoiding was the one I most needed to make. I was nervous when I clicked on the number in my contacts. Not a week earlier I had entered "New Boss!" to the list. Guess I'd have to delete that one.

"Paul, this is Seth," I said. I explained my situation, dreading his response. But Paul—or Mr. Positive as I'd soon think of him—didn't miss a beat.

"Seth, don't worry about the job. It'll be here when you're healed up. Get better and come in when you can," he said.

Did I really just hear that? Relieved, I relaxed back into the hospital bed and started counting down the hours until I could get out and get to work. On day three, the nurse brought my discharge papers. It would take some time for the cracked ribs to heal entirely, but at home I was able to give all my girls a big hug, and it felt great. Feeling better, breathing better, and excited, I rested up for my first day of work.

I rode in with Steve, and while I had been there once before, my focus had been on getting the job, not the place itself. As we pulled in at quarter to eight, I looked around. Picture an auto dealership—polished showroom floors, high ceilings, beautifully decorated interiors, a lot with neat rows of clean cars glinting in the sun. Well, this was not that. To say that a used, semi-truck dealership does not carry with it the same prestigious air that a new car dealership does is an understatement. The huge lot was entirely filled with used semi-trucks, several acres' worth at least. It took me a moment to see a break in the rows and rows of trucks where a plain, flat-roofed office building stood. It looked like a double-wide trailer or a prefab industrial building. Off to the right and near the property line stood a tall, old two-bay garage and behind that—well, more trucks. Steve and I walked up the worn steps to the back door. "You ready?" he asked.

I was nervous. Aside from being a warm body, I didn't have much to offer by way of sales experience. At least, not selling trucks. "I have no idea, dude." Steve laughed, and I followed him inside.

He gave me a tour that lasted three minutes, tops. Two main halls along the perimeter with another running down the middle, and office doors lining both sides. *At least we have private offices,* I thought to myself.

At eight sharp, I followed Steve into the conference room. Everyone was sitting around a giant, laminated mahogany-colored table. "I see you're feeling better!" Paul exclaimed with a big smile. I wanted to take the chair in the corner, but with a little welcoming pat on my shoulder, he pointed me toward an empty chair between a couple of other guys. "Everyone, this is Seth," he said before I'd even had the chance to sit down. I felt like I was in kindergarten…or at an AA meeting. Several said hi, a few others nodded in my direction. Paul motioned toward a taller guy with a maroon polo and a clean-shaven face. "Seth, this is Jim. He'll show you the ropes." After that, he went around the room asking each person for specifics about deals they were working on. In less than a half hour, he adjourned the meeting, and an administrative assistant walked in with a stack of new-hire paperwork for me to sign. "Come see me when you're done," Jim said. "We've got an office for you."

After two hours of signing my name—two hours!—I went to find Jim.

"All done with the paperwork," I said.

Jim smiled, then guided me to a middle office. No windows, no natural light, no nothing. It looked like the war room in some third-world country. There was just enough space for a desk and a cabinet. As for the desk, it looked like it would take just one more sales guy casually sitting on its corner before it would collapse. On top were a phone, a computer, and a few notepads.

"This is called the hole." Jim chuckled as the words came out of his mouth.

I shot him a confused look.

"Basically, we throw all the new guys in here until they can prove they're worth keeping."

I relaxed. I can sense sarcasm a mile away. I was going to like this Jim guy.

"Here's what you need to do," he said. "Use that phone to call companies interested in what we sell, then put all of the information into our system."

My eyes got wide.

"Joking, dude," Jim said. "Come on, and I'll show you what you need to know."

That was the beginning of my informal but excellent training. Paul knew what he was doing when he chose Jim to show me the ropes and get me started on selling. Not only did Jim know his stuff, he was a kind, patient person, second to none. He had to be patient with me, because I barraged him endlessly with questions. "What's that? And how do we do that? And why?" I had no idea about anything he was teaching me, but I was excited. This was my chance to save my family's house. It would take a lot of work, and I'd have to catch on quickly, but I could do it. The day flew by. When I jumped into Steve's car, my head was smoking.

"Well, how was your first day?" he asked.

"Dude, you can make a lot of money if you play your cards right!" Steve smiled and slowly nodded. "Yes, you can."

At home, Desirea wanted to hear all about my day. She loves details, and I didn't disappoint.

"So, do you think there's a chance we can keep the house?" After all our recent financial troubles, she was awestruck by the possibility.

"I do!" I replied. A nerf arrow whizzed past my head, and I heard the unmistakable laughter of my oldest daughter. She ducked behind the corner. "Sorry, DZ, our conversation will have to wait!" My daughter giggled from her hiding spot as I ran toward her. The chase started in the hall, but like always, it ended in the living room, with both of us grinning as we squared off on opposite sides of the table.

Desirea looked on with amusement. The possibility that we could stay in our home—what a relief after all the pain of the last months! "Seth," she said, "that's incredible news. How are you going to do it?"

Our daughter shot towards her bedroom with playful screams and I followed. "I have no idea, girlie," I shouted out behind me, "but I'm going to figure it out!"

From that day on, I rode with Steve to work every day, making sure I was standing by his car ten minutes before we had to leave in the morning. He became just as important a mentor as Jim was, answering my endless questions and giving great advice during our thirty-minute commute. At the office, I got to know the other sales reps, and I never shied away from asking them how they found success.

"Talk to as many people as possible until you find someone who is willing to buy. It will happen," some of them said. "You'll do fine."

From others I heard, "Be polite on the phone and tell everyone that we're the best. Keep at it, and you'll do just fine."

"Be super positive, and you'll do fine."

"Smile before you pick up the phone to make a call. The customer will hear it in your voice. Remember, be positive!"

"And I'll do fine," I said.

"Right! And you'll do fine."

My big take-aways were:

    1) Make lots of phone calls

    2) Tell customers we're the best at what we do

    3) Always be positive

How simple this was going to be!

I saw right away that the guys making the most sales pounded the phones hard and beat the streets more than the others, all while conveying a positive attitude toward the customers. I was inspired. Every day, I walked into the office, sat down at my rickety desk, and started dialing. But after fifty voicemails and ten hang-ups, smiling became a little difficult. The next day, the same thing. And the day after. As the days came and went, my balloon of optimism started to deflate.

"Sales is a numbers game, Seth, don't give up!" I don't know who said it; it was 8:15 a.m., and I had my head down, focused on the phone calls I was making and the deals I desperately needed to get. I'd been there for a month and had nothing to show for it—not a single sale. I was discouraged, but I refused to quit. I pounded my fist on my desk and told myself, *Today is going to be my day!* I paused to take stock of the wobbling desk, forgetting it was living on borrowed time. Nothing collapsed, so I picked up the receiver. For the next three hours, I called, had conversations, and left messages… lots of messages. Nothing.

Needing a break from disappointment, I walked into Jim's office.

"Hey, there," I said, plopping down in a chair. He motioned for me to wait as he finished typing something—probably a sales order, something I hadn't yet had to do—and I leaned back in the chair, raising the front legs off the ground as I gazed at the ceiling in a stupor. After one last click of the keys, Jim asked, "What's up, dude?"

I looked at him but remained silent. My mind was numb. He tossed me a foam football. I tossed it back. After a few moments, I came out of my trance.

"Jim," I said, "I'm making all these calls, I'm smiling while I do it, I'm keeping it positive, but there must be more to it. Is there something concrete that I could do or at least some words I could duplicate over and over again that would work?"

He threw the ball toward the ceiling and caught it over his head. "Not really. Know your inventory and let the numbers play out. You'll get it." He had taught me a ton, and for that I was appreciative, but to hear the job wrapped up so tidy and neat didn't sit well with me.

"Thanks, brother," I said, trying to hide my dejection. Gotta be positive! I leaned forward, and the front two legs of the chair dropped back down to the worn carpet. Back in my hole of an office, I picked up the phone and began the routine again. As usual, I didn't make a single sale.

"Well, babe, do you think you're catching on?" Desirea asked that evening as she handed me a glass of iced tea. We were standing together at the kitchen island. The girls were outside playing.

"I don't know, maybe I'm not cut out for this." I regretted having to say it, but it was the truth. Maybe sales wasn't my thing.

Desirea looked at me closely. "What do you think isn't working?"

I laughed. "Me," I said. "Me. I'm not working!" My laugh died out quickly. "I know that some of the guys have more deals, but I've been chalking it up to experience." I downed the iced tea in one long gulp. "I would just think that by now, I would have something, you know? The way everyone talks, it's almost like it's luck of the draw, and I keep coming up short."

My supportive girl walked around the kitchen island to console me. "Keep after it, you got this," she said, giving me a hug. I had to smile; it was the second time that day I'd heard that.

The next morning we all took a seat around the fake mahogany table for our weekly sales meeting. "Seth, you got anything cooking?" Paul asked.

God, this was getting painful. "No, sir," I replied. I wished I were on a rock somewhere instead of admitting failure in front of the entire sales team. A tall, vertical rock. Climbing. I knew I was good at that.

I caught a glimpse of Steve across the table. He kept his eyes down. Not only was I failing my family, but I felt horrible that Steve had vouched for me.

"Hmm," Paul responded, then moved to the guy to my right. When the meeting was over, I stood up, slowly shaking my head. "Well, I guess I'll try again today. If I keep at it, something is bound to happen." That's what the other guys said, right?

Nothing happened. Not that day or the days that followed. In fact, every day was becoming Groundhog Day. Coffee, check the news, shoot the crap with anyone who wasn't ready to work, check inventory, call a few people, get nothing, smile when Paul asks how I'm doing, play Candy Crush on my phone, make a few more calls, plan where to eat lunch, go to lunch, be grateful there's no clocking in or out for that, walk back to the office, talk to anyone who walks by, call a few more people, listen to someone else get a deal, get pissed off but also, strangely, get motivated by it, get disappointed that it's not working, it's three o'clock and time to start winding down the day (which is a talent, to wind down something that was never wound up in the first place). The next day, repeat.

A few weeks more of this, and Mr. Positive turned into Mr. Serious. "Hey, shut that door behind you," Paul said, after calling me into his office. I sat down in the chair without being asked.

"What you're doing isn't really working, is it?" Here it comes, I thought. I'm about to get fired. I nodded.

"Have you ever thought about outside sales?" he asked.

What? I'm not getting fired?

I'm not getting fired!

"No, sir," I said, "but Jim took me out on some calls when you first hired me."

Paul tapped a pencil against his desk as he thought. "Waiting for the phone to ring isn't working out. I suggest you use your time to do something more proactive, don't you think?" With that statement/question, Paul lifted his head and shot me a look. The message was clear. Make something happen or I'd be out.

I nodded. "Yes, sir, I will."

As I stood up to open the door, Paul said quietly but firmly, "Something needs to change, bud."

I didn't even turn around as I walked out. I felt a wave of shame wash over me. He'd taken a risk on me, and now he was losing confidence.

I changed up my sales tactics right away. No more sitting by the desk all day. At least twice a week, I'd go out and find my customers, face to face. A few days after Paul's talk with me, I was on the road heading east, about forty miles from the office. I found the rural road I was looking for and soon pulled up to a decent-sized cattle operation. As the cloud of gravel dust settled, I caught a whiff of hog crap. In front of me was an old single-wide office. Behind me were about fifteen trucks.

"Can I help you?" a middle-aged man in a flannel shirt, stained jeans, and a cowboy hat asked when I walked into the office. He had a southern drawl and looked the part of every farmer I had ever seen.

Nervously, I began my pitch. It all came out in a rush. "Hey, my name is Seth and I sell trucks and I saw you had some trucks and thought that you might need some more trucks and if so, I would love to sell you those trucks. We, as a company, have been selling trucks for a really long time so if you need any trucks, we have those trucks and yeah, ummm…here's my card."

I think he almost chuckled, but knowing that I must be inexperienced, he showed some pity. "Well, I appreciate you coming out, and I'll keep you in mind."

I stood up to leave, and he followed me to the door. You would think that with me barely making it through that verbal exchange, I would have been eager to get out of there. But nope, I wasn't done humiliating myself. "Nice looking International trucks," I said, complimenting him on the fifteen or so trucks outside. He cocked his head sideways a bit and his mouth opened as if to say something, but he stopped and just nodded.

I hopped in my car and as I backed away from the building, I glanced over at his line of trucks. Kenworths. Not a single International among them. I felt my face go red. I was still stewing in my own embarrassment when my cell phone rang a few minutes later.

"Seth, this is JD." JD was a potential customer I'd called a few weeks earlier. "I had a truck go down, and I need a replacement right away," he said. "Can you help me out?"

"Yes, sir!" A flood of emotions washed over me, and they must have landed on my right foot, because I couldn't stop myself from speeding the rest of the way to the office. Overwhelmed with nervous excitement, I sprinted down the hall yelling, "I got a sale, everyone!!!" It was at that moment that I became a believer: Get in front of people and eventually, it will work out. Just like they'd been telling me.

"Hey, girlie, I'm about to sell my first truck!" I said over the phone. I had called Desirea as soon as I got to my desk.

"That's awesome, Daddy."

"Hey, sweetheart, can you put Mommy on?" My daughter giggled, and I heard the phone hit a table. Two long, empty minutes passed before I hung up. Telling Desirea would have to wait. I finished the deal that afternoon and when the clock hit five, I couldn't get home fast enough. I was jacked! I opened the door and the smell of burgers hit my nose.

"I heard you sold your first truck today. I can't wait to hear all about it," Desirea said with a big smile on her face. She saw my look of surprise. "I was told," she said, giving a little wink to my youngest, who was smiling from ear to ear. I laughed.

Desirea's kindness never ceases to amaze me. We were broke, I was all but failing at a job, and yet, she wanted to celebrate the day with me. As she poured out drinks and dished out the burgers, I told her and the girls about the events of the day. When I got to the part about my stupid comment at the farm, we all had a big laugh.

"It's funny," I said. "But maybe I need to know my inventory better. Maybe even think of myself as more of a consultant."

Desirea almost choked on her burger, which caused a chain reaction of giggles from our girls. I knew why DZ was laughing. She and I had talked about the kind of sales reps who get defensive and say, "I'm not a sales rep, I'm a consultant!" It had become an inside joke, yet here I was, thinking perhaps that's exactly what I needed to be—a consultant to my customers. It wasn't about what I called myself—I didn't care what word or term I applied to the job I did. I just knew that I needed to elevate my game, and this was the logical place to start. Looking around our table from left to right, I had smiles from my pregnant wife and my girls. It had been so long since we had laughed as a family that I had almost forgotten how much I treasured those moments. I remembered now, and that was all the motivation I needed. I wanted more days like this.

The next morning I was quick to shut my office door and get to work. Only now, instead of making endless sales calls, I fired up my computer to search for everything I needed to know about the trucks I was selling: product knowledge, industry trends, our processes, and what makes a truck a good truck. Class was in session, and I was both teacher and student. Inspired by the emotions of the past twenty-four hours, I became a sponge, soaking in all the information I could find. Knowledge was my new weapon; at the very least, I'd never have a repeat of what had happened with that farmer the day before. And what about the sale I had made? Had it been the result of luck, or was it the result of some solid sales principles I was only now figuring out?

Who cares? I thought. *I made a sale!* That meant I had done something right, which meant that I could do it again. I was on my way.

There was a learning curve over the next few days, but once I got it down, I eagerly looked for the opportunity to share my newfound knowledge with any and every customer. It was almost fun! What customer wouldn't be impressed with my intelligence and "consultant" approach? As soon as they saw how knowledgeable I was, they would have to buy from me, right? I knew I was on the right track, because the more I learned, the more in-depth my conversations with potential customers became. It felt great! I could understand and even add to almost every discussion with ease. Furthermore, I was gaining more respect from my co-workers.

In my research, I learned that recent data showed it took an average of eighty-seven calls to sell one truck. No problem, I'm on it! But, wait, I'm confused. I could have sworn that last week data said it was only seventy-four calls, and a few weeks before that, it was one hundred and thirteen. The formula was there, but it seemed a little muddled. I didn't care, though, because now I knew the formula (sort of). I was putting the time in, making the effort, proactively (funny how that word is used so much in sales) learning about my product and my customers. I had it figured out!

A few days later, with no new sales made, my burst of motivation burned itself out. Still, I knew as I slipped back into my normal routine that I was getting better as a salesman, that as long as I approached every day with the sincere hope that "today was the day," something cool was going to happen. And a couple times a month, it did. With a wife ready to give birth any day, I had become a guy who sold two or three trucks a month, and I was perfectly comfortable with it. Hey, it's better than selling no trucks at all! Maybe I wasn't killing it, but at least we had some income, and, miraculously, considering the debt that had piled up when I wasn't making any money, we were still living in our house. Those pie-in-the-sky deals that I would make a fortune on…well, I would just have to get lucky. And I believed I would—eventually.

FOUR

I Would Never
Admit This, But...

IN THE PAST FEW years, I had grown from doing novice climbs to serious, extremely challenging ones—the kind that even experienced climbers walk away from. It took a great deal of physical training, but I was starting to see that it was my mental preparation that gave me the confidence to keep pushing forward. I hadn't yet figured out that this same kind of mental preparation was crucial to improving as a sales rep.

After our daily sales meeting one Monday, I was outside throwing the football with Jim when he threw the dang ball on the roof. I gave him a scowl. He laughed.

"You know, Jim, other than having to climb up to the roof to get your stupid football, do you know what I can't stand about this job?" (Full transparency: I kind of liked climbing to the roof to get the ball.)

"What is that?" Jim asked.

My hand was already gripping the rusty metal conduit running from the electrical box up the side of the building. I started up the pipe and within seconds, I was mantling over the top of the roof. I flipped the football down, then edged downward along the conduit. On the ground, I answered. "Every other job has always been the same. If the job is to remove a shed, I remove it. Then after that, I get paid. Even with climbing, I know what needs to happen to get to the top. Once I execute it, I'm there. In short, the outcome is controlled." The pipe had left a trail of rust on my dark blue shirt. As I tried to brush it off, Jim said, "I understand that, but if you can get good, it does happen consistently."

I gave him a smirk. "Well, I guess I'm not good yet." Walking toward the back door, I stopped. "You know, the reason sales kills me is that I just can't get comfortable with the concept of 'do what you're supposed to do and then hope.' It absolutely kills me, dude. Seriously, is there no control over a paycheck? That is messed up." I didn't make any sales that day, or the next.

During those first months of not selling anything, I had been discouraged. Now that I was selling, but not much, and not with any kind of system that seemed to make sense, I had hit a new level of discontentment. In its way, this stage was worse than the one before. Back then I'd been working from a sense of desperation. Now, desperation had turned into just-barely-comfortable, a far more dangerous state of mind. No matter what I tried, I wasn't figuring out the sales game. If something didn't change, I would be stuck here forever, the two-sales-a-month salesguy.

I wanted more, and I didn't know how to make that happen in my current position. I didn't give up completely, but I did start looking for a new job, and I'm pretty sure I sent more resumes in a week's time than I made sales calls. One morning, I got a response from a potential employer. I jumped up, shut my office door, and sat down to call them.

"Yes Seth, we're looking for someone to change tires here in our Nashville, Tennessee, location. We pay fourteen dollars an hour to start."

Would moving my family out of state for fourteen dollars an hour be a good idea? At least it would mean I could quit the sales job.

Fourteen dollars an hour—what the heck was I thinking?!?

Wrong question. The more accurate question would be, what was I feeling?

The answer: depressed.

I didn't take the job. And thanks to some good acting skills, I was able to hide my true feelings about my situation from Paul. Each month, I convinced him that this month would in fact be THE month. It's a shame that I wasn't as good at selling trucks as I was selling a load of crap to my boss. I just wished it were five o'clock already.

"Seth, they scheduled me for this Thursday," my wife informed me over coffee one Saturday morning.

"That's awesome!" I replied. I set my cup down and leaned to wrap my arms around her before moving them down to her belly.

"I already let our parents know, so we should be good on sitters," she continued. I nodded. She was always the planner.

"Cool!" I said. "I'm excited!" She was going to give birth in a few days' time—of course I was thrilled. But underneath was the nagging question of how I was going to support the family.

Thursday arrived, and in the car on the way to the hospital, I turned to Desirea. "Are you ready for this?" I might have been asking myself the same question, or maybe I wanted some kind of re-assurance from DZ that everything would be alright. She had the happy glow of a woman about to have a baby, but I sensed a current of unease similar to my own running through her. We were ready, we were excited, but our financial situation wouldn't allow us any mental peace.

"Of course. And so are you," she said, giving my hand a reassuring squeeze.

Hours later, Desirea gave birth to a beautiful little girl. Baby and mother were doing great, and the hospital discharged them that day. Back at home, we passed the baby from family member to family member until well after dark. As I kissed my sleeping wife on the head that night, I smiled at my newborn, peacefully sleeping in her mother's arms. What a perfect day. I was grateful that I had the next day and the coming weekend before I had to return to my chamber—err, I mean office. When I did, it would be with a new sense of gravitas. That little girl, just like her sisters had done, stole my heart. Her arrival grounded me and motivated me to continue on.

We humans are creatures of habit. And so, the best way to predict the future is to look at the past. Remember what I did when my world came crashing down? Remember where I was when my truck got stolen?

"It's close to here," I said to myself, tapping my pen distractedly on my notepad. It was 8:15, and I was already bored. I leaned back in my office chair and made a deal with myself: If I called fifty people before lunch, I'd let myself slip out and go climb. Once again, I felt grateful for not having to clock in or out. If I got back a little late from climbing during my lunch hour, no one would notice. Everything I'd learned about sales was that it was based on luck. If I didn't have any control over the outcome, why not go somewhere and do something where I did? Besides, climbing was a lot more enjoyable than dialing the phone. I made my fifty calls and left.

With my crash pad, shoes, and chalk in the trunk, I drove fifteen minutes to the little crag where my truck had been stolen. I hadn't returned since, and even that memory couldn't dampen my joy to be out there. I quickly grabbed my stuff from the back of the car and headed towards the trailhead. The path wove left and right beside protruding boulders; for the most part, the trail was so worn that you couldn't get lost even if you wanted to. "This is home," I said as

I gazed up at the two-story granite monsters that surrounded me. I say "monsters" because I knew this specific spot well, and it was a shoe-eating, finger-destroying place that never let up. The rock was loaded with sharp granite crystals, smears, and divots. There will be blood, I thought as I looked at the formations around me.

I had already climbed the same old popular routes in front of me. I wanted something new. Far to the right and well off the main trail, I caught a glimpse of a fifteen-foot-high, crazy little arete that started off overhanging and then halfway up leaned back in. I hopped over a root and walked over for a closer look. It was featureless and awkward. It stole my heart.

Reader, picture an outside corner of a house but tilt it back a little. After about eight feet, the outside corner rounds off, and as it morphs into the outside of a barrel, the tilt returns to normal; towards the very top, it even slants in a touch. That's just what this rock looked like. It was so awesome. No doubt others had climbed it, but I certainly hadn't seen anyone attempt it. I was riveted.

I threw my crash pad underneath the corner and plopped down to stare skyward and visualize the approach. The start would only be possible if I pressed the center of my chest squarely on the edge of the corner. While there, I would attempt to get purchase with my palms on either side of the corner, pushing as hard as possible while my fingertips pressed into the crystals. If that wasn't enough, I would have to position my feet in a way that they would stick to the granite without sliding. In short, a lot of things would need to come together perfectly for this to happen.

I returned to the office that day without so much as a single effort to get on the wall. Instead, I had used my lunchtime visit to carefully plan my route, and in doing so, my mental focus had shifted. My mind wasn't on selling a truck, it was on tackling that climb. So I made another deal with myself. Fifty calls every day before noon, and I would be free to return to the crag at lunchtime.

After two weeks, I had figured out which muscles to tense and which position every part of my body needed to be in to get off the ground. Despite this, and despite having the strength to pull off the opening move, after a couple hundred attempts, I still wasn't making any progress. This objective—to get off the ground—was becoming all consuming, and I realized how much I missed this kind of challenge. How much I missed the addiction of being in control of an outcome. The more I tried and failed, the more I wanted to figure it out.

Several hundred attempts later, I was back at the rock, but this time, I changed up the approach. Holding myself steady, I took my hand off the rock, reached out to the right, and grabbed a small but sharp edge. It worked! Progress!

I would not get past that move for the next couple of months.

Winter came, but in the South, that isn't a deal-killer when it comes to climbing. During the summer, the heat would soften the soles of my shoes, and they would leave a long black, greasy stain on the rock when they slid off, a visual scoreboard announcing another failed attempt. Now that it was colder, the rubber of my shoes stayed sealed to the almost non-existent ripple.

I knew that my failure to climb the rock wasn't from a lack of effort; every day I returned to the office with layers of skin missing from my fingers. Most days, instead of chalk on the holds, a sea of blood trails marked the start and stop of any progress I made. I wasn't upset about all the failed attempts; I was sincerely confused about what was going wrong. I talked to myself, played mini-movies in my mind, and it even got to where I could accurately tell which muscle would be triggered to fire in sequence, but none of it was resulting in success.

I'm not sure why I started to question the opening move again, but I assume it was out of desperation. Was there another way to start this that would put my body in a position that allowed me to free up a limb to find the next hold? I spent another entire lunch hour sitting at the base and observing the route. Then I shifted my focus to the entire rock; was there another way? I began experimenting but got the same results. I failed, and the next day I failed again, and the day after that, too. Why in the world would I keep trying and failing with different approaches when I had found an opening move that worked? I realized that no matter how hard I tried to climb this boulder, this particular start wasn't going to get me to a place where I could continue upward. Knowing this, I had two choices: quit or figure out a new approach.

I plopped down on my crash pad and once again focused on the rock above me. The same familiar starting holds that I had stared at so many times were evident, but on this particular day, my attention shifted, and I spotted something off to the side. There was a light layer of moss that I had never paid attention to before. I grabbed my brush and within a few minutes, I had the entire area scrubbed completely clean. Now, with the green blanket of moss gone, the secret I had been looking for revealed itself: a small dimple that had that classic granite stickiness to it. "Oh, dude! It's on now!" I whooped, elated. Two attempts later, I flung out to the edge with no problem. To make it better, I didn't resemble a pretzel when I hit that hold, so I was free to fire again. "Woo hoo!" A couple more attempts and I threw a heel hook out left and freed up my hand to reach for the next edge. I say "edge," but really it was more like a subtle dish or another little divot. Either way, press friction was going to be the only way to stick, so, being more than pleased with the progress and with my fingers starting to leave blood trails once again, I called it for the day.

The next morning was busy. I delivered a truck and followed up with my phone calls. At 11:45, with just two steps left to the door and my lunchtime climb, someone behind me said, "Hey, Seth, where you going?"

I turned and saw Paul.

"Good job this morning," he said. "Want to grab some lunch?"

Well, crap. I always enjoyed time with him, but my whole motivation for the day was to get back to my rock. "Sure," I said, hoping my disappointment didn't show.

At the restaurant, Paul asked about my family and how things were going in general. That's the thing about Paul; he genuinely cared about his employees. He was the kind of manager that made you want to do well just to make him proud. Oh Paul, if you ever read this, please understand that while I fully realize that it wasn't responsible for me to miss so much work, I assure you that you didn't lose a penny from my truancy. The only thing you lost was a warm body sitting at a rickety desk making phone calls that resulted in nothing. That being said, thank you for not firing me. It would have been well deserved, even with my two or three truck sales a month. My head was not at work, it was at the rock. Speaking of that...

The next day was sunny and clear with temperatures in the mid-thirties—perfect climbing weather. This time no one was around to stop me from slipping out at lunchtime.

There was just one impossible-looking move that stood between me and the upper, slabby top. To paint the picture, let me first explain the movement. I would have to press the tip of my middle finger into the rock so hard that the sharp, small granite crystals would imbed into my skin. That was my right hand. I would leave my left hand free as a counterbalance, while both of my feet would be smashed together on a slant barely a quarter inch wide. The face of this rock was completely vertical, which meant that with one uncontrolled breath, I could lose purchase on the rock immediately. And I did, many, many times. Thank god for my crash pad.

What I needed was to grab far to the right, close to the corner, and slap a little ripple without losing balance. If I could accomplish that, I could raise my left leg into the air while pressing my left middle finger into the same crystal that my right had vacated. Once that was done, slowly and methodically, I could then place my left leg on the smallest of divots and fire up strong with my left finger.

Confused?

Yeah, me too. Besides that, the move was bloody. Words do not describe how awkwardly I landed when I didn't hit it just right. It was do or die as far as the attempt went, and for several weeks, I did the latter.

Then one day, that changed. "Ahhh!" I screamed, as my middle finger jammed perfectly but painfully on that crystal. *Oh my god, oh my god, this is happening*, I thought. I shut my eyes and slowed my breathing to a stall. Unbelievably, I was sticking. My entire body was shaking uncontrollably as my eyes shot from one toe to another. No part of me was secure. *Oh my god, what do I do now?* One last desperate and balance-y move stood between me and the upper, slabby sections, but I was at a loss. "Breathe, brother, you got this," I said to myself. I breathed in and cautiously moved my right foot up. Just then, I threw my hand towards a blob of rock as hard as I could. Slap! I got it!

My fear turned to joy as I quickly tiptoed up the last few feet. "I freaking did it!!!" I yelled, pumping my fist in the air. No one was around to hear me, but I didn't care. I had given so much of myself over the last half year to these fifteen vertical feet. My body turned to mush as I collapsed and buried my head into my arms. "I made it, I made it!" I repeated over and over to myself.

Sitting atop my world in that euphoric moment turned bittersweet as I realized that my challenge was officially over. That boulder had been my purpose, the one thing that I had to do. Looking back on it, it's one of my proudest achievements. For the first time ever, I absolutely refused to not succeed. It took discipline, mental strength, and even a fair amount of blood to fail over and over again.

But through it all, I never questioned whether it was attainable. It wasn't a matter of whether I would succeed or not, but rather how.

Packing up and driving back was a blur, but I was still giddy as I walked down the hall towards my office. I certainly wasn't in the head space to pound the phones or to "be proactive," so I shut my door, sat down, and admired my old rickety desk that by some miracle was still standing. The old desk and I both had something to be proud of.

"What an accomplishment!" I said aloud as I leaned back and shut my eyes to go over the climb in my mind. I recalled the first moment I had seen that little boulder, and how I had visualized myself standing at the top without having a clue how it would happen (or how long it would take). I remembered that from the beginning, I knew it was going to happen, that one day I would be standing on top of that boulder. And today that had become a reality.

My eyes flew open. *Hey!* I thought. *I've done this before.* Every time I had to push the boundaries to conquer a new climb, I started the same way: by picturing myself standing on top. I internalized the emotions, the strength, and the overall wow factor of being able to actually do it. In short, when I finally reached the top of something, it usually was the second time I had been there; the first was when I'd gone there in my mind.

My thoughts traveled back to those first few moves. I'd spent so much effort trying to get past the first move. Sure, getting off the ground was progress, but immediately afterward I was completely shut down again. After replaying countless failed attempts in my mind, I realized what had held me back. It was my focus. I had been focusing on trying harder, when I should have been focused on my technique. There isn't a world where trying harder would have gotten me past that dead-end. Trying harder wasn't the problem—my technique was. It wasn't until I had reset my thinking and changed my entire approach that I had a chance to progress. All of this wallowing in success and replaying my awesomeness got me thinking about work. Partly because Paul popped his head in to see how my day was going.

"Doing great, Paul! Couldn't be better."

He shot me a confused look, and I gave him an enthusiastic nod. He had seen the sales sheet. Blank.

I went back to my thoughts. I felt as though the climb were trying to teach me something. If I'd learned a lesson on the stone, was it something I could apply to sales? Is sales really just a numbers game? Is the secret really just calling on as many people as possible? Is it really just a matter of luck and hope and being educated about the product? About being smooth with the customer and firing off closes with confidence? If so, why wasn't I doing better?

One thing I had learned for sure was that those questions were in response to ideas. In this case, I wondered if the ideas weren't better defined as educated assumptions. True, the educated assumptions were made by people more experienced and smarter than me, but did that mean they were correct?

We've all heard them. *Smile when you pick up the phone to make a sales call. Be positive. It's a numbers game. The only thing that leads to success is more effort.* In the world of selling, these platitudes are seen as the definitive practice for selling. They've certainly stood the test of time. But what if people believe in them not because they're correct, but simply because they've been around so long? As the new guy, I supposedly wasn't qualified to question their wisdom. But that was before my battle on the rock. Now I was seeing things in a new light. And that light involved examining the old assumptions.

Now that I was really thinking about it, it seemed that some of these assumptions—some of this sales advice—sure did a good job of softening the landing when someone underperformed. I laughed out loud as I recalled the many times I had defended losing a sale:

"There was nothing I could do, the customer just wasn't ready."

"I thought that this was going to be a great month, but things just fell apart."

"Hey, some customers can't get financed, nothing I can do about that."

"The price was too high."

"The market is soft."

"The product didn't meet the customer's needs."

And on and on.

Thinking back on it, I realized it was a rare occasion when I took complete ownership for my results. Unless they were good. Then I had no problem owning it. But missing a sale? I passed the blame for my own underperformance like rolls at a dinner table.

Going back to that climb. It had taken a lot of work to find the initial first move, and who would have blamed me if I had stuck with it instead of looking for an alternate start? After all, that successful first move had gotten me going on the rock. Maybe it didn't get me any farther along than a few feet off the ground, but that was through no fault of my own. What if I hadn't wanted to trade that small success of getting on the wall for the bigger payoff of finding another way, one that would let me keep climbing past the first few feet? Lots of people would say there's no value in undoing a successful start and redoing it some other way. Right?

Enough! I thought to myself. *Enough thinking for the day, Seth.*

But the idea was planted in my mind just as firmly as my finger had been stuck in that divot. Just like I had decided to question the start to that boulder, I had to question my strategy on sales. "I'm doing everything I can to sell and I'm putting forth every ounce of effort that I can," I mumbled, as if defending myself against an invisible opponent. I'd said something along these lines a million times—to Paul, to my wife, to past bosses. Now, I thought back to my boulder. My response was incomplete. What I needed to say was, "I'm doing everything I can to sell *the way I know how* and I'm putting forth every ounce of effort that I can *without starting over and trying something completely different.*"

With that, I turned back to the phone. A few dozen calls left before quitting time.

FIVE

Down I Go

"THERE'S A LETTER TAPED to our door, Seth." DZ's voice on the other end of the line was calm. Pinning the phone between my shoulder and ear as I walked down the hall, I slipped into my office and shut the door behind me.

"A letter?" I asked, my stomach dropping. I knew without her telling me what it was, but I needed to hear it. To know I wasn't in a nightmare that I could wake from.

"An eviction notice."

I sank down into my chair. "How long do we have?" I said, my voice barely above a whisper.

"Two weeks."

It was inevitable that this day would come. It had been a year since we came home to the first eviction notice, and since then we'd been fighting hard to send money to the bank whenever we could. I shut my eyes, my mind whirring. In front of my monitor was a notepad where I kept information on all the deals I was currently working on. I took a glance. None of them were due to close anytime soon.

"Okay, girlie, let me see what I can do."

The thing I most needed to do, I couldn't bring myself to do—the news left me too distracted to focus on sales calls. I walked to Paul's office. "Hey, Paul, can I take a personal day?"

He barely lifted his eyes from the report on his desk. "Sure."

I hated leaving, but I needed to get home. I could only imagine what Desirea was thinking and honestly, we needed to figure out together what to do next. When I pulled into the driveway, she was there waiting for me. She had downplayed her sense of panic on the phone, but I could see how upset she was. As soon as I hopped out of the car, her arms were around me and her head was buried in my chest. I dreaded seeing all our remaining possessions tossed onto the front lawn, but that was minor compared to the bigger problem.

"We're going to be homeless," Desirea said, sniffling.

I put my hands on her shoulders. "We can't afford much, but we can afford something. We've just got to find it," I said in what I hoped was a reassuring tone.

She nodded. Inside, we each grabbed our laptops and Desirea handed me a glass of ice water. We sat down at the table.

"Okay, let's find something," she said hesitantly, shooting me a genuine smile. Maybe it was going to be alright after all.

An hour later, the only affordable "something" we found was in an area where the school district made the news more than the weatherman did. We widened our search.

"The only decent houses I see are more than an hour's drive from Atlanta," Desirea said. Our oldest came in from school. Oh man, it was already mid-afternoon! We'd been at it for hours with nothing to show for our efforts. We took a break to hear about our daughter's day, and Desirea pre-heated the oven for dinner.

"Hey, what about this little place!" I said, pointing to a small, cabin-like house with a wrap-around porch located halfway up a wooded mountain.

It was the first house I had found, so Desirea jumped up optimistically to stand behind me. "Seth, it's in north Georgia. That's got to be two hours away."

I acted like I didn't hear her comment. "Look at the pictures of the view from there. It's unreal! Want to go see it, girlie?"

She shook her head, but she was smiling. "Sure."

That very evening we got our three girls packed into the car and drove the two hours up to the house, arriving just before dark. The place was vacant. After we walked the perimeter together, we decided that this would work. I don't remember my logic, but somehow I'd thought that moving far away from the city would increase my sales. And if that happened, this little rental would be perfectly affordable. A quick call to the landlord and we had this place locked! We were moving.

It was a relief. While it was sad to think of saying goodbye to our friends and our current home, the eviction had turned our house into a ticking time bomb. The prospect of starting over someplace new felt good.

By that weekend, we had our things packed and by the next, we had moved in. Oh, it was heaven. The town was small and safe, the schools were good, and we had an endless supply of mountain streams, waterfalls, trails, and never-ending views. The highest peak in the state was directly in front of us, and every morning it was like a dam had been released as the fog flowed into the valley below. Drinking coffee in the morning on the back deck was the highlight of our day.

I loved living there, even with my two-hour commute each way to the office. Somehow, though, the daily four-hour commute didn't result in more sales—surprise!—and rent ate up over fifty percent of my bring-home every month. Before long, we found ourselves in a different place, same situation. Basically, all we had done was to kick the can down the street. One thing about that game: No matter how hard you kick the can, eventually you catch up to it.

One evening Desirea and I were sitting on the back deck after getting the older girls to bed. The sun had just dipped below the mountain to our west, and darkness was settling in.

"Do you have to go in tomorrow?" she asked as she rocked our baby in her arms. We'd been watching the lights come on in our sleepy little town below and listening to the crickets rev up for their loud nightly performance.

"Yes," I said.

She nodded but didn't say a word. Now that we were down to one car, she and the girls were stranded on this mountain every time I left for work. Even worse, I had started staying with Chris for two or three days during the week to save on gas money. Desirea and I both hated it, but there was nothing we could do. She rocked back one last time before using the momentum to stand up. With our youngest cradled in her arms, she tiptoed to the crib. After checking the lights, we took one last look out the blinds to ensure our car was still there before we turned in ourselves. Yep, we were still on the watch-out for the repo man.

We painted our new life in the most positive light for anyone who asked, but the underlying problem was still present. Financially, we were living on the edge.

After a few months in our new place, my parents made the trip from up north to see us. I had scheduled my Atlanta time so that I could be home when they arrived, but a meeting with a customer ran late, and thirty minutes after my parents arrived, there was a knock on the door. When Desirea opened it, she saw two middle-aged guys.

"We're here for a vehicle, but the one in the driveway doesn't match the description," said one of the men.

Desirea quickly stepped outside and shut the door behind her.

"My husband has it in Atlanta," she whispered. She looked through the window to make sure my parents weren't paying attention.

"When will he be back with it?"

Desirea shrugged her shoulders. She didn't trust herself to talk without starting to cry. They must have taken pity on her, because they left without another word.

As if being broke and living in a strange town with three children wasn't enough for my warrior of a wife to handle, now we would also be losing our only remaining car. She sobbed as the men drove away. Inside, my parents heard her.

Being an adult, it was not easy to accept help from my parents, but I had no choice. They bought us a cheap but drivable vehicle from an as-is lot. Anna, as we named the car, was a ten-year-old, hunter green mini-van with two hundred thousand miles, a drooping headliner, flat seat cushions, and no AC or functioning windows. She drove great aside from the few times that she didn't, which, unfortunately for us, seemed to always happen in the mountains. Anna didn't give me many problems, but Desirea was behind the wheel when the brakes went out and again when the timing belt broke within weeks of each other. Desirea and Anna had trust issues, but either way, we were grateful for my parents' generosity.

I can assure you not one day went by that I did not know I was absolutely failing my family. Despite our hopeful start at our new home, things had gotten worse, not better. One autumn morning, my mother-in-law drove to our house for my daughter's first birthday. A child's first birthday is supposed to be special, but the best we could do was a measly celebration in the corner of a Wendy's with a few dollar-store gifts we didn't even bother wrapping. Desirea's mom didn't say a word, but I was so humiliated that I couldn't look her in the eye. How horrible it had to be for my wife. We were so broke, and here I was, the guy who couldn't support his family despite leaving them alone and without a car for days on end. Leaving to work, but yes, also to play.

Brutal honesty here: Hanging out with Chris during my work trips in Atlanta was a release from my hell of a reality. Climbing, disc golf, adventures, good food—all the fun I was having was good for my soul and helped keep me mentally above water. Meanwhile, my wife and girls were home alone and without a vehicle. I still cannot fathom the millions of thoughts that must have been running through my wife's head while she sat alone and isolated on the mountain, while I was off working and having fun. At the time, I didn't see how I was running away and making horrible decisions. Desirea and I didn't argue, but the gaps of time between our calls grew longer with each trip I made.

"Hey, Seth, we need to figure out this tax thing," she said on the phone one day. "The girls and I can get a ride to the city if you can meet up."

"Sure, girl. Absolutely."

Her choice of words should have tipped me off to the growing dysfunction in our relationship; you don't just "meet up" with your wife like she's a long-lost friend. We basically had been living two completely different lives, and the reality was that we were slowly losing our ability to fight—for survival, for hope, and for our family. It had been a few days since I'd seen them, and when they showed up at her sister's house, hugging Desirea felt awkward. It was weird. In the kitchen, she pulled out some tax paperwork and pointed to where I needed to sign, and afterward we cooked outside and ate dinner together. We didn't have much to say to one another; the time together felt somehow empty. The next morning, I stood quietly in the corner and watched them get ready to leave for home. I was at a loss. As Desirea climbed into the car she'd borrowed from a friend, our eyes locked. Neither of us said anything, but it was as if we exchanged a thousand words in those brief seconds. The car backed out of the drive, leaving a plume of gravel dust. It didn't hit me until that moment: I'm going to lose my family.

If you're thinking that was rock bottom at that point, you're wrong. In early December, a few weeks after that weekend, Desirea called me at the office. She was crying. "Have you checked our bank account today?" she asked.

"No, sweetheart." I was puzzled. We didn't have much, but I knew it was enough to cover rent with a few hundred left over.

"Well, the IRS just cleaned us out. We have nothing."

"Nothing? It's all gone?" I really thought losing the house was the last tie to my failed business, but this latest gut punch blindsided me. Instantly, the reality of our situation sank in. We were screwed.

"Yes, gone. Guess I'll see you…whenever." She hung up. Her response summed up her hopelessness. I was devastated.

And stuck. Suddenly I wanted nothing more than to get home, but with no money in the bank, I couldn't use my debit card to fill the tank. All I wanted was to be with my family. I shut my office door and googled "how to contact the IRS." Hours later, I still hadn't found what I needed. I crossed my arms in front of me on my desk and buried my head on the inside of my elbow.

I don't understand his magic, but Paul always had a knack for knowing when something was wrong with his people. He came in, sat down, and said, "What's going on?"

That was enough to release the floodgates. I allowed myself to get emotional not only with another dude, but with a boss for whom I had consistently underperformed. Now that I was talking, I didn't hold back anything. Paul listened without judgment, occasionally murmuring a sympathetic "mmm" or saying, "Gosh, right at Christmas time and you have a young family." When I finished, I was depleted. Paul gave me pat on the back when he left my office, and I returned my head to my arms. My thoughts were accompanied by a few tears. What a hopeless day. I could only imagine what Desirea was feeling, stranded and alone.

"Hey," I heard. It was Paul. "Whenever you're in a position to pay me back, I know you will." He dropped a personal check on my desk. I couldn't believe what I was seeing. I had told him how much the IRS had withdrawn, and now he was giving me a check made out for the exact same amount.

It was a big slice of humble pie to accept money from my boss, but it was only because of this act of kindness that I could get home. I had to work the very next day and I had a two-hour drive in front of me, but my mind, my emotions, and the universe itself were all telling me that I must see Desirea and my girls right away. It was the longest two hours of my life. When I arrived, there was no awkward hug and no awkward silence. I put my arms around Desirea, and we spent the next few hours talking. For the first time ever, we openly admitted how miserable we were and how badly we wanted things to change. It was a turning point for both of us, and we knew it. We were committing to turning things around, no matter how hard it would be. We were ready to fight and most importantly, we were resolved to let nothing stop us. The next morning, I had to wake up before dawn, but I didn't mind. With renewed hope, I kissed Desirea and the girls goodbye and made the long drive back to Atlanta.

Two weeks later, my parents visited again for Christmas. Desirea and I didn't have the money to buy gifts for the girls, but my parents hauled in a pile of wrapped presents and placed them under the tree. Words can't describe how much that meant to me. Desirea prepared a French toast casserole for the next morning, and everyone went to bed happy.

Unfortunately, when I rolled over in bed early the next day, I knew something was wrong. "Desirea," I whispered.

"Hmm?" she said sleepily.

"I think my lung collapsed again."

"Really? Are you sure?"

"Pretty sure, girlie."

Desirea was awake now. "What do you want to do?"

I didn't want to ruin our Christmas celebration. "I'm going to try to make it through this morning and then I'll go to the hospital." She tried to argue, but I had made up my mind. An hour later, with the delicious, sweet smell of the casserole filling the house, we had breakfast and then took our seats to exchange presents.

"Girls first," I said, trying not to wince at the pain in my chest. The little girls smiled and dove into the massive pile of unopened gifts. I was having a hard time breathing, and minutes felt like hours. But when the girls were done, I pointed to my parents. "Your turn." I wanted them to have a nice time; the hospital could wait. After that, the only gifts left were for me and Desirea.

I reached out to take a present from my mom and a stab of pain hit me. I decided it was time to let my parents know what was going on. "Hey, ummm, this morning I woke up to a collapsed lung again," I said, trying to keep a neutral tone so they wouldn't worry. It must have worked, because my parents didn't seem to react.

I tried again. "Yeah, I guess my lung collapsed again."

This time it got their attention. In a moment, my mom and dad were at my side. "Seth! What are you going to do?"

Desirea, without saying a word, got up and started packing a bag for both of us.

"I need to go to the hospital," I said. They were still in shock but immediately offered to watch our girls.

As it turned out, the small bag Desirea packed wasn't big enough. My condition was more serious than we thought. Two surgeries later, my beautiful wife and I celebrated the New Year with cups of hospital Jello as I lay in bed, full of tubes and IV lines. They'd had to remove part of my lung and put sticky stuff on the inside of my rib cage to keep a deflation from happening again. When I was released after two weeks, I had an extensive recovery ahead of me.

SIX

A Defining Conversation

DRIVING THE LONG MOUNTAIN road back to our house where I would rest for the next six weeks, my attention returned to our financial situation. Feeling guilty, I turned toward my wife. "Hey girlie, do we have enough to keep us afloat?"

Desirea shook her head. "You don't need to worry about any of that, you just need to get better."

But over the next weeks, with nothing but time on my hands, I couldn't not worry. Thoughts of money, or rather, thoughts of the lack of it, took center stage.

Finally, the day arrived when I could return to work. I didn't mind my two-hour commute at all that February morning. Nothing but smiles pulling in, going inside, and talking with my colleagues. Obviously, they knew what had happened but were curious about specifics. After an hour of mindless chatter, I finally made it to my office. I shut the door, smiled at my poor battered desk, and got ready to make a plan for the day.

Just then, I heard a knock and in walked Paul. We greeted each other with a smile. He stood, his hands on the back of the chair that sat across from me. "Seth, I've got some news for you," he said. "I've been asked to move to Kansas City. It will be happening pretty quickly. I wanted to let you know."

"But I just got back! That sucks!" I said, stunned.

"I've been wanting to get back to Missouri, and this is my opportunity."

I was crushed. I really liked working for him.

"It's been great working with you," he continued. "And I'm sure our paths will cross again."

After he left, I thought about it some more. It really did suck, and not just because he'd been a good boss. With my sales record, I couldn't imagine another boss being as tolerant or patient with me. Paul had clearly liked working with me, but would his replacement?

I fired up my computer and settled in to work. Within minutes, my phone rang. It was a man I'd called on before.

"Hi, Seth. I'm in need of six trucks. Can you help?"

I paused and forgot to breathe. My heart was racing. Was a multiple truck deal seriously about to land in my lap? It turns out, yes, it was, and one with a ton of gross profit! After we got the details worked out, I couldn't help myself—I drove home to tell Desirea the good news in person. With all of the horrible and painful conversations we'd had the last year, this would be a welcome change. I pulled into our gravel driveway, and my feet barely made contact with the ground as I flew to the front door. Inside, my wife and girls were sitting on our worn green couch watching TV.

"What are you doing home?" DZ asked as she stood up with a confused look. The girls jumped up and gave me a hug. As usual, they weren't quick to let go. My wife would have to wait for an answer, but I was confident it would be worth it. As my girls excitedly told me all about their day, she kept shooting me perplexed looks.

"I would have made you a plate if I had known you'd be home."

"No need, girlie, I'm not hungry. I just wanted to see you."

Desirea laughed. "We just spent the last two months together. Don't give me that." Out of nowhere, her face morphed from confusion to concern. "Oh, god." She walked over and whispered in my ear. "Were you fired?"

I smiled but said nothing. This was the first time in several years that I felt like a hero to my family, and I was enjoying every minute of it.

"Nope," I said with a grin. "But I did sell six trucks today."

Desirea's hand shot up to her mouth. I could see tears pop up in the corners of her eyes. "Are you serious?" she asked. I nodded. Once again she buried her head in my chest, but this time, it was a warmth like no other.

The commission check came, and it was crazy high. What a thrill! Paul was due to leave for Kansas City in a few days, and the first thing we did was repay him the money he'd so graciously given us in our darkest hour. Then we paid off all our bills. It felt great, even if there wasn't much left over from our windfall. For the first time in well over a year, we were out of debt. It was fantastic.

Now that we had a little more breathing room, financially speaking, we decided this was our opportunity to move back to Atlanta. Just to be clear, the breathing room does not mean that we had money, but it did mean that we didn't have to check the mail for overdrawn letters from the bank.

In mid-March, on the morning of our anniversary, I got up early, started a pot of coffee, and went in to wake up Desirea. "Happy anniversary!" I said, jumping on top of her. We had a big day planned.

"I'm up, I'm up," she said, rubbing her eyes and stretching her arms over her head. While she got dressed, I poured coffee into to-go cups and woke the girls.

"Where are we going, Daddy?" they wanted to know.

"You're going to your great-grandma's house," I answered. I smiled as I carried the last travel bag out to Anna. Two hours later, the girls were tucked away at Desirea's grandparents' house, and my wife and I had the day to ourselves.

"Happy anniversary, dear," DZ said, as she shot me a loving smile. I returned the same. "You have the list?" I asked. She pulled out a piece of paper. On it were the addresses of all the potential houses we could afford. "Let's get our family back together," I said.

We spent the entire day driving around and looking at houses for rent. We didn't have money for dinner and certainly not for gifts, but that day would go down as my all-time favorite anniversary ever. We had an entire day alone with each other, and we talked about what we had been going through. At the same time, for the first time in so long, we were in the financial position to do something about it. What a perfect way to celebrate our marriage!

By six that evening, we still hadn't found anything to rent. Despite the wonderful day, we were both feeling sick with disappointment. We had driven over a hundred miles as we jumped from city to city. What if all our hope came to nothing?

"I hate to admit it," I said, "but we might have to return to life as normal on top of that godforsaken mountain." It was getting dark, and we were heading back to pick up our girls. We were both exhausted.

Just then my phone rang. "Seth, my name is Luke. You called about the house I had for rent."

It took me a second to remember which one: a split-level at the end of a cult de sac fifteen minutes away from DZ's grandparents. "Right, thanks for calling back. Is it still available?" Desirea had pressed her cheek against mine to hear the conversation.

"Yes, it is. When would you like to see it?"

Desirea pulled away from me and began moving her arms up and down excitedly. She was mouthing something silently, and I could read her lips loud and clear. "Could we see it tonight?"

Pause.

"Sure! Fifteen minutes okay?"

Our exhaustion disappeared as I turned the car around to head back in the direction we'd just come from. Out of everything we had looked at, this house had been our favorite. Now, all I had to do was sell Luke on why he should rent to a guy who not only didn't make much money, but also one whose credit was in the toilet. Oh crap, I had totally forgotten about needing a security deposit on top of the first month's rent.

In the end, the landlord agreed to rent to us, and Chris loaned us the upfront payment. Chris, my brother, thank you. You didn't just help us move back home—you saved our family. A month later, we were settled in. Yes!

None of us knew him, but we heard a little about Paul's replacement before he showed up at the office. Jason was supposedly a competitive, hard-driving boss who was usually dissatisfied with sales results, even if they were good. We were nervous.

"Seth, come to Jason's office." It was his third day when I heard the summons via the intercom. *Oh boy*, I thought, as I made my way down the hall. Three of my co-workers were already standing in front of our new boss's desk.

"This will be short," he said. "I've been looking over the data and you're all underperforming. Unless I see a big change, I cannot allow you to keep taking up space here."

We looked at each other uneasily. I could tell the other guys were pissed. I figured before the day was out, they'd be practicing darts with his picture as the target.

As for me, I was taken aback by how direct he was, but I also knew he wasn't completely wrong. After two years, I should have been doing better at sales. Aside from my recent six-truck deal, my results had been poor. There were some legit reasons why my performance was so bad, but judging by Jason's tone, he wasn't open to hearing excuses, so I bit my tongue.

"That's all," he said, turning back to the reports in front of him. We all looked at each other in shock, then made our way out the door.

"What the hell? Screw it, I'm out!"

I turned to see who had made the comment and as I did, I heard someone else say, "Me, too!"

Whoa, I thought. *This is crazy!* Still, there was no way I was going to walk out on my job now that we had our new house, and I was able to be with my family every night again.

It wasn't until Desirea and I were washing dishes after dinner that night that I told her about the speech from the new boss. She listened without saying a word.

"You got this, Seth. You should talk to him, but don't give him excuses about why you haven't sold more. Ask for his help. Any boss would have to respect that."

I nodded. My girlie knew what she was talking about. Still, I had a restless night as worries played out in my head. While driving in the next day, I decided to take my wife's advice.

"Jason? Can I have a few minutes of your time?" I half peeked my head in the doorway of his office.

Jason smiled. "Absolutely. What's up?" I was surprised by his cheerful tone. Had he forgotten about our last conversation?

"Umm, sir.... I could use your help. With sales. I want to get better."

He waved me into a chair next to his desk, turned off his computer, silenced his phone, and got up to shut the door. He was giving me his full attention.

"Tell me what you're thinking, Seth." The gentle, caring tone was a far cry from what he'd used in our talk yesterday.

"What you said to us yesterday? I've been mulling it over. And you were right. I've been underperforming. And I want to sell more."

"Seth, let's get down to the basics. I assume you know why you're here and what you want. So, why haven't you gotten it? What's holding you back?"

I had the sensation that I was being pinned into a mental corner. There was no escape.

He asked question after question, getting more specific with each one. They weren't questions I hadn't heard before, but his style was one I'd never encountered. With each answer I gave—about how the market had taken a dive, or how we had priced this or that truck too high, or how our credit checks were getting in the way—he sat and listened silently. The more he stayed silent, the more I talked, because, well, silence is freaking awkward. At the same time, I was seeing my answers in a new light, consciously weighing what I was saying more than I ever had before. When I had finished dumping every reason imaginable for my poor sales in his lap, he smiled again.

"Seth, can you answer my questions instead of ducking them?" He wasn't angry at all. His tone was friendly, which added to my confusion. "I guess from what you're saying," he continued, "it's not your fault that you can't sell more, correct?"

Silence filled the room. I didn't understand his question completely, but I knew I didn't like it. And I knew that not liking it didn't matter. Message delivered, message received.

Back at my desk, I continued to think about our conversation. He had forced me to reconsider my sales efforts, to see them in a new light, one that involved taking far more personal responsibility for the outcome than I was used to doing. I had been saturated in the conventional sales mentality for such a long time that I had become another victim of it. But all his probing and prodding directly supported what I had been questioning about sales all along. When he asked that final question about who was to blame, he wasn't expecting an answer. He was planting the seed for a new way of thinking. And it worked. It was time for a change.

That night on the way home, I stopped and bought a book on selling. I hadn't been much of a reader before this, but that first book turned into a landslide. Books-A-Million and Barnes & Noble got any extra cash I had as I gobbled up new material. Yep, after my talk with Jason, I committed to waking up an hour early every day to saturate my mind with everything there was to know about the art of selling. I started with easy books, titles by Brian Tracy and a few others, then leveled up to Stephen Covey and beyond. Tracy's books laid a foundation of thinking, and Covey's books got me interested in human psychology, which birthed an obsession about why people do what they do (yes, I read that book, too). This was exciting. My knowledge was growing, and I could feel myself changing far more quickly than I thought possible.

One Sunday during church, my wife pointed at a pamphlet. "We should join a small group," she said. "It would be good for us to meet some people." She could see I wasn't thrilled. Meeting new people in a group is awkward. "Seth," she said, shooting me The Look. "We're going."

I reluctantly signed us up for that Thursday, and Thursday came too quickly. When I got home from work, DZ already had the kids ready to go.

"Let's just try it out," she said.

Ah, walking into the home of someone you've never met before. It triggers a chain reaction from your head to your feet. Your brain tells you to smile big and find humor in something, anything at all, that anyone says. I was smiling, but I wanted to be anywhere but there.

"I live less than a mile from you!" said a guy named Michael. He and I had been chatting for a few minutes, and he seemed like a cool dude. He shared my odd sense of humor and, like me, he had an active lifestyle. "We should run together."

Running is much easier when someone else is there to encourage you, and the added accountability would be awesome. "Sure, Michael."

Soon we were meeting every day at five in the morning, and that five a.m. commitment blossomed into a great friendship. Michael was the manager of a car dealership, and we had so much to talk about most days that the run ended long before the conversation did.

The momentum had shifted back to Desirea and me, as we were much happier as a family living closer to the city and most importantly, living together. I still climbed some weekends, but aside from that, camping, canoeing and soccer with my girls filled the majority of my free time. There was more of a balance in life, and soon, I lucked into being a three-to-four-truck-sales-a-month guy, which gave us a little cushion financially. We were no longer in the red— we were pink. Dark pink, but pink nonetheless.

I continued devouring sales books, but after a while they all started to sound the same, and I could sense where they were headed long before they ever got there. It all made perfect, logical sense, and most of the principles were simple. However, what I was learning, painfully, was that any learning curve, no matter how simple, has stages that cannot be bypassed. These skillful authors got the information into my head in a ton of different ways, and that was a good first step. But the next steps were on me. I had to reflect on how to apply those concepts to my world, how to launch these new weapons of mass influential construction in real life. My early attempts failed miserably. I would be ready to close a sale, and somehow instead I'd push the detonator on a bomb. If that sounds destructive, well, it's an accurate description of how it felt.

Though I was failing—though not as miserably as earlier— something about trying out these new ideas gave me a sense of purpose similar to the one I had with climbing. Attempting to figure out sales consumed my thoughts. The main question I kept coming back to was: How can I predict success in such an unstable profession?

One morning on my run with Michael, we were approaching lap number two when he started telling me about work the day before. "Man, I am so frustrated with one of my sales guys," he said. Michael never got upset about anything, so I was curious.

"Why is that?"

The sun was just starting to rise over the far field in the park, and Michael slowed down to a walking pace. "He has the talent, but if he would just shift his focus, he could be a rock star." The next thing he said I will remember until the day I die. "He focuses on results, which leads to hope. But if he would focus on the right behaviors instead, he'd get the results he wants."

Remembering the "try harder" approach that would have never worked on my boulder, I contemplated this new way of looking at results and behavior. His statement spoke to me. Perhaps my greatest obstacle in sales wasn't in having all the right answers, but rather where I put my focus.

On the way to the office, I reflected more on what Michael had said. How did it apply to my particular world of sales, to selling trucks? I thought of all the same questions I heard over and over: What is your sales goal for this week? This month? How many truck sales are you shooting for this year? How many calls will you make? How many emails will you send? On…and on…and on. I began to connect the dots. Those questions focused on *what I hoped to accomplish*, but what I needed to focus on was *how to accomplish it*.

A note from the author:

An unbelievable light bulb went off in my head on that morning run, a light bulb that changed my life. From selling a few trucks a month to selling more than I could count; from driving Anna, the clunker, to being able to afford new vehicles for me and DZ; from barely making rent to buying a home of our own; in short, from financial worry to financial freedom. I wish I would have learned these lessons earlier, as it would have eliminated so many years of pain. Or perhaps I needed the struggle to appreciate the new insight? (The old saying, "Some have to pee on the electric fence to know that it's live," comes to mind.)

By now, I hope you have a good sense of my journey. But I didn't write this just to tell my story, to share the pains and humiliations I experienced in the early days of my career. I wrote this to share a solution.

The remainder of the book is devoted to doing just that. Told through stories about rock climbing and about climbing that much trickier wall—selling—I'll share with you what I discovered. Over the next chapters, I'll describe four sales principles, and in alignment with those principles, a repeatable, trackable, and proven sales strategy. I hope this makes your journey smoother than mine. Ready? Let's get after it!

SEVEN

Begin with the End in Mind

– or –

What I Learned from Free Climbing

WITH FREE CLIMBING, you scale a rock without safety gear—no harness and no safety line. You're doing the same moves as with a regular climb, but the difference comes from knowing there's nothing to break a fall except the ground below. This gives the experience a whole different feel. Free climbing is about as real as it gets. Maybe that's why it got into my head that I wanted— scratch that, I *needed*—to free climb something tall. Just thinking about it had my stomach in knots. But it was something I wanted to prove to myself—that I could overcome the fear and do it.

I finally got my chance one weekend in Georgia. DZ and I had rented a cabin for a little family trip, and fifteen minutes away was a mountain with a tall exposed rock over a hundred feet high. On our second day there, I slipped out of the cabin at five a.m. and arrived at the base of the mountain before sun-up.

"This is it!" I said aloud, looking at the face of granite in front of me. As my feet hit the trail, my mind, as usual, clicked into movie mode. With each step, I played a film in my head, a visualization that started with me standing at the top of the wall of rock, victorious.

Wow, it's going to feel amazing! I thought to myself.

Then, "This is crazy! Why am I doing this? What if I fall?"

"NO!" my mind yelled. The trail crossed over a lazy stream, and the tranquil sound of the water had a soothing effect.

As I played the moves in my head, I welcomed the emotions that would soon be rolling over me, and I determined how I would handle them…over and over again, like a movie on a loop. Each time I replayed the imagined climb, my fears got smaller and my confidence grew. "You got this!" I yelled into the forest. I hadn't told my wife I was going to free climb—I didn't want to worry her, and besides, what if I didn't follow through with it? But to the uncaring trees around me, I shouted out my commitment. I was going to free climb my way to the top.

Around the bend, boulders the size of houses filled the gullies, and ferns covered the ground on each side of the trail. Shades of gray and green saturated the landscape, punctuated with the occasional pop of a yellow flower.

Huffing and puffing, I arrived at the opening where the tree branches parted. A few steps away, the dirt trail led up to the side of the rock. Go time! I assumed the position, then began my scramble up the forty-five-degree angle. These are the moments that make me grin, even when I'm sweating my way up to a granite wall I'll climb with no partner and no safety.

After seventy feet, I sat down on a ledge and quickly changed my shoes. Above me, the forty-five-degree angle straightened to a clean, brutal ninety degrees. Straight vertical. Standing again, I looked upward as I wrapped the chalk bag around my waist. The gray granite wall stretched as far as I could see to the left and the right. And the top? It was so high I couldn't see it.

Without so much as a thought, I started the ascent, following the moves that had been playing in my head. Right foot up and stand. Shift weight to the left, place toe on a ledge barely a quarter-inch wide. Breathe in slowly and grab a hold. Repeat.

With my core tense, my quads burning, and my fingers straining as they latched on to the rock, I was more than thirty feet off the deck before I looked down. "Oh, my god, I'm really doing this!" The feeling of climbing with no safety wasn't just enjoyable. It was empowering.

Earlier, when I'd been thinking about the climb, I had been nervous and even a little afraid. But now that I was physically committed, I wasn't scared at all. In fact, I felt euphoric. I looked over my shoulder to see the huge valley far below. My head was spinning as I shut my eyes and breathed in and out several times. From the parking lot where I started to where I now stood had to be a thousand feet. This was surreal.

I turned back and continued to climb. Hand over hand and step over step, as I gained elevation, the movement became less of a climb and more of a dance. My breathing was controlled, every muscle was disciplined to fire at my command. And then, before I knew it, I was topping out over the edge. I gave out the loudest howl ever—I'd done it! My first free solo, and it had been a beautiful, flawless ascent.

I don't recall what went on inside my head during the forty-five-minute hike back to the car, but true joy was at the center of it. I'm sure some scientist or doctor would have an explanation of why climbing ropeless made me so happy, although I wouldn't understand it. Physically, it hadn't been as demanding as some other climbs I'd done. Clearly something else was at work here, something besides pure adrenaline.

Then I realized what. The "aha" moment hit me hard.

Hiking toward the wall, I had replayed the mental movie over and over. It started with me standing on the top of the rock, the climb successfully completed. And then it unfolded in reverse, with all the specific moves it would take to get to the top. I had internalized each move and mentally examined any issue that might get in my way.

And the "aha" moment?

I suddenly understood that having such a clear vision of what standing on top would look and feel like had changed my mindset. My mind was focused solely on fulfilling my vision, and every physical move was merely acting in congruence with that thinking.

Lesson learned: *How we visualize the course of action determines how we think about it, and how we think about it influences how we behave.*

Core Principle 1: Begin with the end in mind.

The end I am referring to here is the only end that matters. It's the ending you create in your mind.

- Why are you here?
- What do you want out of this?
- How does this end?
- What does success look like to you?
- What will success feel like?

Oh, the joy of having such a clear picture! I am going to ask anyone who is willing to take just a moment to walk through those questions and really seek out the true answers. Don't get stuck thinking about the various ways you might fail; pretend that your success is a given, guaranteed. This will allow you to clear the decks of your mind for the important mental exercise of picturing each step leading you to that success. Create the mental movie, and don't leave out a single detail.

I promise this isn't another fluffy motivational practice. I'm not trying to convince you that we can all be billionaires. I would never do that to you, reader. These are your thoughts, your dreams, and your vision. Think of what you want and picture it as a jigsaw puzzle. No matter how intricate or how many pieces, the first step is to stand that puzzle box upright and have a close look. If we don't know what the finished puzzle looks like, how can we possibly know how to connect the pieces? This is vital. We must have a clear picture of what it means to succeed. Where there is no vision, people perish (that might be Biblical).

Hey, how helpful would it be if the picture on that puzzle box was blurry or pixelated? Not at all, right? Just like that box, we need to stand our vision upright to guide our mentality and actions to our chosen end.

EIGHT

Focus on Behaviors, Not Results

– or –

*What I Learned
from My Daughters*

M Y GIRLS WERE NO strangers to the outdoors. Starting from the time they were little, I had been showing them climbing moves and had even let them do a little climbing themselves, but purposefully, I had kept their exposure to a minimum. Until now. I surprised the two older girls with a camping trip after work one weekend with the plan of teaching them how to rappel. This wouldn't be just a physical challenge for them, but a mental one. More than I had bargained for, as it turned out.

"Dad, we're up so high!" my oldest cried out.

"What?" I answered jokingly. When we had arrived the night before, it had still been dark, and the girls' moods were bubbling with expectation. Now, lying on their stomachs and peering over the top of the cliff in the early morning daylight, they looked terrified.

"The safest anchor is a big tree," I explained as I wrapped the rope around the trunk of a tree growing out of a crack on top of the cliff. "If the anchor is secure, it's really pretty simple. Put a carabiner and a belay device in the main loop of your harness." I latched the carabiner to the yellow harness my oldest was wearing. "Make sure the rope is running in where it's supposed to, then walk backwards while keeping the other end of the rope down. Make sense?"

She nodded nervously.

"See how safe it is?" I continued. "With someone standing on the ground holding the rope, it's almost impossible to have an accident." I smiled in encouragement, but my oldest's eyes remained wide with fear. It took some cajoling, but I finally got her to take the plunge over the edge.

Within seconds, she was consumed by fear. "I want to be on the ground already! I want to be down!" she yelled in a mild panic.

This was going to take some cheerleading on my part. "You're doing great, girlie. And no need to yell, I'm right here." She was barely three feet away from me. "I want you to get down, too." Wrong kind of cheerleading. Her eyes filled with tears.

I explained the process once again and reassured her that she was safe. "You need to loosen the rope just a tad, and then you'll start to descend."

"But I want to be down NOW!"

After a few more minutes of gentle encouragement, I convinced her to ease up on the rope and she dropped—two feet. The tears were coming fast now. More encouragement, and she went down another couple of feet. I kept reassuring her, but after an hour my beautiful girl had descended barely twenty feet. Suspended in the air for that long with her right hand in a vice grip on the rope was quite the endurance test, but her will to survive what she assumed was a deadly situation was winning out.

She kept looking over her shoulder and then back to the rope. "I just want to be down!" In a calm voice, I explained to her that if she kept focusing on getting to the ground, but didn't take action to do it, she was never going to get there. "Focus on what you need to do, and I promise, you will be on the ground before you know it," I said. It must have sunk in. She turned away from looking over her shoulder and nervously peered at her hands holding the rope. Slowly but surely, she let out the rope, and within five minutes, her feet were on the ground. She had accomplished more in those last five minutes than she had the entire previous hour.

Still, her terror hadn't gone unnoticed by her younger sister. When it was her turn to rappel down the cliff, she was having none of it.

"Can I climb down here instead? So I don't have to do the rope thing?" she asked, pointing to the ravine at the side of the cliff.

That's right, reader, my little girl decided it would be safer to climb down the ravine without a rope! She took one look at the ground far below and then shifted her attention to where to put her feet and hands. Without my advice, she repeated move after move, and in five minutes she was down. I followed behind, and holy crap, was it treacherous. How in the world she kept herself together, I will never know. "I just kept looking for the next spot to put my foot and hand until I was done," she explained afterward.

Wow. I learned so much from my girls that day. Thinking about it back at the campfire, it reminded me of what Michael had said about his salesman: "He focuses on results, which leads to hope. But if he would just focus on the right behaviors instead, he'd get the results he wants." My oldest had hoped to get down to the ground and was laser-focused on just that—*being* on the ground. Her sister wanted the same thing, but she focused on what she needed to do to get there.

Lesson learned: *It's easy to dwell on what we want to happen, but focusing on how to make it happen is the only way to achieve success.*

Core Principle 2: Focusing on results leads to hope, but focusing on behavior leads to change.

In sales meetings, we're asked what our goal or target is, and it's common to answer with a number. "This month I'm going to sell X number of trucks (or widgets or whatevers)." If that's how it is for you, I'm certainly not judging. I used to answer in the same way.

But I learned a different way that day with my girls.

Yes, I needed to start with the end in mind, but that was just the beginning. For progress to happen, I needed to focus not on the end itself, but the behaviors that would get me there.

The questions in those sales meetings would stay the same, but my success changed when my answers did.

Interlude:

The O.R., My Dream Climb

On the southeastern portion of the Blue Ridge mountains in North Carolina, an uninhabited valley lies nestled between a thousand-foot rock wall on the left and a gentle sloping mountain on the right. This mystical place is not full of fields, but rather jam-packed with an assortment of massive hardwoods that practically touch the sky. As with any mountainous terrain, the trees above hide the story of what is happening down below. Underneath the canopy of these living skyscrapers, the terrain is riddled with waterfalls, streams, and huge drop-offs. Due to the elevation, Laurel trees with their signature waxy leaves grow in abundance, and the predominant color is the deepest green imaginable. As the valley floor rises upward, the ground grows steep, until hundreds of feet higher, the dense thicket of trees, bushes, and vines thins and disappears. All that remains is the most beautiful, imposing wall of stone in the region. For over a thousand vertical feet and as far to the right and left as one can see, the wall dominates one's visual field. Along its light gray face run occasional black streaks, as if someone dumped tar from the top. Massive blocks and pillars rise from the base for hundreds of feet. The place looks prehistoric and angry. One feels very, very small standing at the base of the rock.

This wild and perfect place stole my heart the first time I saw it. Reader, if you're in the climbing world, you might have heard about this hybrid. It's called the O.R. If not, there's no need for me to spell out the whole name or give its exact location, because honestly, we all have our own O.R.s—big, impressive, fear- and adrenaline-producing rock walls we feel compelled to climb. From the moment I saw it, I was entranced. Climb it, I must.

NINE

Hope Alone Is Not Enough

– or –

What I Learned from a Climbing Legend

"THIS IS A BUCKET LIST item for sure," I said to Desirea as we sat on the couch. It was the day after I'd seen the climb of my dreams on my way home from work. "I've heard stories about it, but yesterday was the first time I've ever seen it in person. DZ, it's incredible!"

She shook her head slowly. She knew how dangerous the place was. "If you plan on climbing it, I hope you get as much info on it ahead of time as you can."

My face cracked into a smile from ear to ear. I had just received permission. I ordered the climbing guidebook immediately, and it arrived a few days later, confirming the rumors I had heard. There were just as many pages devoted to discouraging climbs as there were describing the routes. Climbable lines that start off promising, only to disappear a short way up; lines that wander hundreds of feet to the left or right, making a retreat impossible. Every route on the wall, including the O.R., was labeled R/X (the "R" rating means you'll sustain a serious injury if you fall, "X" means you'll either be seriously injured or killed in the case of a fall). Storm cells, the book said, could hit anytime without notice, even on the sunniest days, making the friction-dependent routes as slick as ice. If you got injured, walking out wasn't an option due to the terrain and length of the walk in. The book showed pictures of helicopters rescuing stranded climbers; the word WARNING was splashed across nearly every page.

Reading this only made me want to climb it more. More precisely, I wanted to lead a climb on the O.R. When you lead, you're at the front, securing the rope to anchor points one section at a time. On some climbs, these points, called "protection," have already been set by previous climbers, but on other routes you have to set them yourself as you scale the wall. The people behind you ride "free," protected by the rope that you've anchored above; as the leader, your only protection is the last anchor you set below. That can turn into a long, hard fall if something goes wrong.

To do this right, I needed to do some serious training. Despite my advanced climbing skills, the confident headspace required to pull it off was above my psychological pay grade. It wasn't a given that I had the physical ability, either. The route was notoriously difficult; I had work to do.

One weekend evening, I drove out to a place near home to climb. I arrived after dark and set up my hammock under the light of my headlamp. Through the trees, I could see a campfire burning with several people sitting around it. I heard the sound of a familiar voice.

"Shannon?" I said, walking up to the group.

"Hey, man, what's going on?"

I couldn't believe it. Shannon, a legend in climbing circles, was camping right next to me! We had done some climbing together with mutual friends in the past, but he didn't appear to recognize me in the dim light of the fire. "You and I climbed together a few times," I said. "I'm Seth."

"Right! Seth. How are you?" He grabbed a beer from the cooler at his feet and handed it to me. "Have a seat, man."

Built solid and strong, both physically and mentally, Shannon was the kind who didn't spend his time at popular climbing crags; instead, he favored remote, unexplored places. But what made him famous was that he didn't care if he had protection (or "pro," as climbers call it). If he saw something that looked fun, he climbed it.

Over the next hour or so, I chatted with Shannon and his friends, talking about past and future climbs.

"Can I ask you for some advice?" I asked. Shannon had climbed almost every route on my dream wall in North Carolina. I told him my plan to lead a climb on the O.R.

"I know it's crazy. Any words of wisdom?"

He responded with a question of his own. "Are you afraid of falling, or are you afraid that you can't pull the move?"

I was blindsided. "I guess I don't know."

Hearing my reply, he halfway laughed and looked at an ember that had strayed from the fire pit. "You need to figure that out, man. If you're afraid you can't pull the move, well, maybe you aren't ready. But if you're afraid of falling, you should overcome your fear and do it." He kicked the ember back toward the fire.

"I can pull the move," I said quietly.

"Then you just need to do it. Stop hoping to do it and just do it."

In my sleeping bag that night, I looked up at the stars and replayed our conversation over and over again.

Shannon was absolutely right. Studying the routes in a book, doing training climbs, and talking about wanting to do it didn't get me to the top of my dream wall. All that want and preparation and hope meant nothing until I put my foot on the rock, grabbed a hold, and started to climb.

Lesson learned: *Hope motivates us, but without action, we'll never attain our goal.*

Core Principle 3: Hope alone is not enough.

Hope is a wonderful thing, and I would never downplay the importance of its role in everyday life. I hope my wife has a great day, I hope the weather stays good, I hope my kids are safe, I hope I sell something today. It rolls off the tongue as naturally and consistently as the sun rising in the morning. Hope in itself is good, but hope by itself isn't enough. It *clarifies* for us what we want but doesn't *get* us what we want. It's crucial to remember that we must take action in order to transform hope into the hoped-for reality.

TEN

Take Ownership

– or –

*What I Learned
from a Friend*

QUITE A FEW MONTHS had passed after that conversation with Shannon, but my focus had not wavered. I was climbing stronger than ever and running laps (doing the same route over and over again) on routes harder than any I'd done before. My palms would sweat just thinking about leading on the exposed, thousand-foot wall. What a gift, then, when I was given the opportunity to calm the last of my fears.

Ian was a climber I had always admired, and I was thrilled to hear his voice on the phone one morning.

"Chris and I are going to check out the O.R." he said. "He told me that you were working on leading it. Want to go so you can put your eyes on it once before you do?"

Ian wasn't just strong and confident; he earned my deepest respect by the way he went about his business. He was humble and approachable. Whether he was talking to a professional climber or a young kid thinking about climbing, he consistently made others feel like the most important person on the planet. I dug that. Dude was always on a different level. And now he was offering to let me ride free on a route I hoped to lead.

"Absolutely. When?" I said.

"This weekend."

"Can't wait!" I hung up the phone, and as we sat down at the table for dinner, Desirea reached over and squeezed my arm. She'd heard enough of the conversation to understand what was going on. "You doing this safely once before you lead it makes me feel way more comfortable."

I nodded. "Me too, girlie, me too."

I could not hide my smile as their car pulled into my driveway that Friday night. Chris and Ian jumped out, and I gave them both a big hug.

"You ready to do this?" Ian asked. He and Chris looked as jacked up about our adventure as I felt.

"Hell, yeah!"

We rode north for several hours before heading east on a road that followed a spring-fed river. As we climbed up mountain after mountain, the river fell lower until it was out of sight. We were still talking nonstop when we pulled into the parking area closest to the trail that led to the O.R.. Around the campfire, our exhilaration turned quiet and more reflective. We admired the clear, dark sky; no pollution or lights to blot out the stars here. It was late.

"Big day tomorrow," Chris said, rising from his chair and stretching his arms skyward. "Time for me to turn in." The last big log had burned down to a gray skeletal cinder.

"Me, too," I said. Ian kicked some dirt over the remains of the fire, and I climbed into my hammock. Sleep didn't come easy. In just a few hours, I'd be taking the next big step to make my dream climb become a reality.

As the rising sun made its way past the thick canopy of trees, I awoke quickly, ready to soak up everything I could about climbing the O.R.

"This is going to be quite a hike," Ian warned as we left the campsite. He wasn't lying. After thirty minutes of down-climbing, scrambling, and pushing thorny bushes out of our way, it was evident why this place was considered so wild and dangerous. When we finally arrived at the base of the route, we double-checked the safety, and Ian started up. Chris and I followed.

Ian was a machine! The route was wilder and more unprotected than I had expected. Just visualizing myself leading this monster sent my stomach to my throat. But Ian confidently ticked off pitch after pitch. "Send train!" he called out again and again, our signal that he was at the top of a pitch and that we could proceed up on the same rope.

The climb itself was beyond enjoyable, but most of my mental energy was spent memorizing each step Ian took: where he moved, where he set pro, where there was no way to protect from a fall, and most importantly, where Ian would say in his calm tone, "Watch me closely." And then, at the end of the afternoon, we were miraculously on top, looking over the edge at what we'd just climbed. What a thrill! We were smiling ear to ear as we made our way along an easy hiking trail back to the car.

"Ian, you must feel like a million bucks," I said.

He threw his pack into the trunk. "Dude, you just have to own it. When I'm leading up there, I make a lot of decisions. And I have to take ownership of any and all consequences. Once you're willing to accept that, the rest is easy."

Chris cracked open a can of beer for each of us. "To Ian, and to owning the route!"

"To Ian!" I said.

Lesson learned: *We must be willing to own failures in the same way we own our successes. Making excuses supports the false notion that we are powerless; only when we take complete ownership can we achieve as much or more than we ever thought possible.*

Core Principle 4: Take complete ownership.

From the moment Ian first rested his right palm on the O.R., the route was his. No doubts, no excuses. It made me think about my upcoming plan to lead the climb. What if at the last minute I lost my nerve and freaked out? What if I decided risking my life was too much? Would I walk away? If I did walk away, I could easily justify it. *Too risky. Irresponsible for a guy with a wife and three daughters.* No one would disagree. In fact, some might even praise me for making the sensible decision! My parents would heave a sigh of relief, my friends would nod their heads, DZ would give me a big hug. I'd be the guy who played it safe, the guy who chose not to do something crazy and potentially deadly. And I'd have to own the fact that I had not led the climb. Own the fact that it wasn't maturity and wisdom suddenly asserting themselves, or a selfless fear of dying and leaving my wife and girls in the lurch, but fear. No justifications, no excuses. Just fear.

We don't usually risk our lives as sales professionals, but there are plenty of ways these two experiences—climbing and selling—overlap. Just as with climbing, there are many variables in a sales job. On any given deal, there can be challenges with the market, prices, customer expectations, product deficiency, supply and demand, money, credit, competition.

A long list of ready excuses for not getting the sale. But excuses, explanations, and justifications, while a balm to the ego, don't grow my bank account. And I didn't get into this business to have my ego soothed. I did it to make money.

It is so liberating to own a personal failure. Owning a failure is a testament of strength, not of weakness. But just as the enemy of great is good, the enemy of complete ownership is almost-complete ownership.

Even if we don't have control of what comes our way, we do have complete control of how we respond to it. Truly examining and acknowledging where we were at fault—how our actions caused a deal to falter—is the secret to finding success. Success is birthed from the ditches of our failure. But only if we are open to seeing and owning it.

ELEVEN

An Experiment

MY CLIMB WITH IAN and Chris was still fresh in my mind, and while I could have happily spent my entire day thinking about it, I needed to concentrate on my job. I spun around in circles in my office chair like a child, hoping to spark a thought. *Aha!* I stopped and quickly pulled a sticky note from my middle desk drawer. Grabbing my pen, I wrote down the four principles that had been taking shape in my mind over the past months:

Core Principles:
- I must begin with the end in mind.
- I must focus on behaviors.
- I must take action because hope is not enough.
- I must take complete ownership.

These were hard-won insights from climbing, but could they apply equally well to the world of sales? Looking at the neon-colored note, I had an idea. Why not call around to some dealerships, pretend to be a customer, and observe their sales process? I typed "truck sales" into Google, picked up my phone, and called the first company listed. Ring, ring…

> Dealership Dan: "This is Dan, how can I help you?"
> Me: "Yeah, I was seeing if you had any trucks around $50k or so."
> Dealership Dan: "Do you have a stock number?"
> Me: "No. Do you have any good trucks around that price?"
> Dealership Dan: "We have some great trucks around that price. Will you be paying cash or finance?"
> Me: "I guess I don't know. What do you have?"
> Dealership Dan: "We have quite a few. Why don't you come down and see for yourself. All of our trucks are professionally inspected, so we pride ourselves on being the best. You won't find a better deal out there than ours. As far as financing, once you pick out a truck, we'll take a deposit and fill out an application. If the bank likes what they see, you'll get the terms, and from there you're good to go. It's that easy. What's your email address? I can send the finance application and links to a few of our trucks."
> Me: "Would you like my name?"

Well, Dan sucked. His questions were rude, and he didn't give a rip about me. I called another dealership and had a similar conversation. The more calls I made, the more intrigued I became. In fact, I didn't stop with truck sales. That day I was in the market for everything: houses, cars, radios, land, even the stock market. I made one call after another, and as far as the person on the other end of the line was concerned, I had a bottomless wallet. I asked the same questions my own customers asked me, hoping I would hear some magical little group of words in reply, a formula or template that I could use in my own sales calls. Did it happen? Nope, not at all. Sure, their step-by-step processes became clear. And apparently I was having a lucky day, because according to everyone I called, they were the best dealer in the state. I don't know how that's possible, but there it was, built right into their sales pitch!

Truth be told, reader, I didn't talk much, as all it took was a question or two from me and the sales reps grabbed it from there. All aboard! Their statement-train was leaving the station, with loud assurances from the overly optimistic, all-knowing, fake-as-hell conductor pretending to care about the passengers. Even if I hadn't been pretending to be a customer, I wouldn't have climbed aboard, at least not with these sales reps.

After each call, I did a quick written review, including how I felt as a "customer." The emotions told the story. The better a sales rep sounded, the more I felt dumb and in some ways, almost like I was a nuisance. I definitely didn't have a better grasp on how to buy what they sold; instead, I came away feeling like I needed to fit into their predetermined sales profile before they would take me seriously. The only thing gained from my little experiment and the ditches of failure was new resolve. I wasn't giving up.

I put down the phone and resumed spinning in my chair. Smoke was practically coming out my ears as question after question about my own sales process shot through my mind.

As a salesman, why do I put more weight on what I say than what a customer hears?

What environment am I creating?

How comfortable are customers talking to me?

Do I want to be right, or do I want to be effective?

"Aha!" I said out loud with a smile, giving my old, dilapidated desk a resounding slap. "It isn't about me and what I say. It's about the customer and how they feel. I should center a strategy around that!"

I thought back to a definition I once heard of strategic thinking: When you say yes to one thing, you're saying no to another. If I say yes to focusing on what is important to the customer, wouldn't I be saying no to focusing on what is important to me? That didn't sound promising. Still, no harm in continuing down this mental path. I got up to close my door, and in the four steps it took to reach my chair, I had an idea. If I was going to build a strategy around a customer, I needed to put myself in their mindset. I jotted down a few questions:

What are they trying to do?
Why now?
What are they after?
What has been holding them back?

I was so focused that a knock on my office door caused me to jump.

"Morning!" Jason called out as he walked by.

A little embarrassed, I blinked a few times to clear my head but swiftly fell back into my reverie. I considered what a customer was feeling when he or she placed that initial call. Their nerves and anxiety must be pretty high. It's not just the purchase of a truck they have to consider. For them, everything has to come together perfectly—the haul source, the type of tags, the commercial insurance, and sometimes, even compliance with local regulations. Sales in other industries come with different concerns, but they all have something in common: an array of issues that must be resolved with the sale of the product.

That being said, it was starting to make sense to me why customers ask for information and then price. I had a theory. Most customers want information and best price immediately. After my little experiment that morning, I could understand why. On too many of the calls I'd made, I had no idea how to buy the product they were selling. Not knowing the right questions to ask, I immediately asked for the best deal.

I was now laughing at myself. As a salesman, I was doing the same thing I'd been hearing from the sales reps all morning. If a customer asked for information, I attempted to build loyalty by explaining our step-by-step process. When he or she immediately asked about our best price, I soft-served the possibility that we would take a deal, hoping it would make me appear flexible. Full disclosure: On a sales call, I often asked myself, *Can I sell this truck even with a hefty discount?*

"Seth, dude, this is your own fault!" I said aloud at my desk. I had been creating and supporting the environment for the customer to exit stage left on their terms, not mine. If I give the customer all of the information up front and suggest that we'll make a deal, what do I have to offer after that? Hope they liked what I said enough to call back? Just then, the neon sticky note caught my eye. Shocked at my own ignorance, I smiled at the answer right in front of me. Hope by itself is not a strategy! It does not put me in control of my own success. My approach was wrong, my thinking was wrong, and I was to blame. I needed a real plan.

TWELVE

Interrupt Thought Pattern
and Redirect

– or –

It's Go Time on the O.R.!

IT HAD BEEN A MONTH since Ian, Chris, and I had scaled the O.R., and I was just as motivated to climb it on lead as I'd been the first day I had laid eyes on it. I called Chris on a warm, spring afternoon. "I'm ready. Are you in?" I asked. Chris and my wife had something in common—they rarely said no.

"Of course!" Behind his excited tone, I heard a note of concern. No doubt he was nervous for me.

"Time kills, brother," I said. "Let's ink this in for Thursday."

Wednesday night came. "I can't believe we're doing this," I said as I threw my gear into his car.

"Dude, me too. Are you sure you're ready?"

I just smiled with a nod. A few hours later, we pulled into the gravel parking lot marking the trailhead to the O.R. I let out a slow exhale. This parking lot was usually a popular spot for the wandering tourist, but late on a Wednesday, not a car was in sight.

"Guess we got the whole place to ourselves," Chris said.

Before long, we were playing a game of chess while enjoying a beer with brats cooked over the fire. It was peaceful aside from the periodic whips of wind that disappeared as quickly as they arrived. Describing to a city-dweller just how crisp and pure the air was is nearly impossible; you have to breathe it in yourself to know the feeling. There was no smog, no noise, no litter, and no city lights to contaminate the night sky. We talked about plenty as we shuffled the chess pieces across the board, but what we didn't talk about was more noticeable: what we'd be attempting the next day. Sure, there were brief mentions, but just like the wind, those words disappeared as quickly as they came. I can promise you, reader, I understood perfectly what I had signed up for. But that evening, it was too big to talk about.

At first light, I awoke to see branches slowly waving back and forth in the light wind above my hammock. "This is it," I murmured to myself. I got up and started breaking down camp. Chris was already awake. "Dude, today is the day!"

He smiled in my direction as he heated up his morning tea. "I'm so excited to be here with you, brother!" His positive spirit was comforting.

After we stuffed the camping gear back into the car, we started up the main trail. The sun hadn't yet made it above the side of the mountain, and a cool breeze hit our faces as we walked along. After about fifteen minutes of easy hiking through the forest, Chris spotted a small pile of stacked rocks, a sign from a previous climber that we were at the access point. The easy part of the hike was behind us. Now we would descend almost a thousand feet.

The little trail grew faint as we found ourselves bushwhacking, down-climbing, and scrambling around boulder piles. After about a half hour, all traces of the trail disappeared. "Dude, are we going the right way?" I was disoriented.

Chris shrugged his shoulders. "I think so."

The remaining path was wide enough for a spider to weave a web from side to side, but not wide enough for me to avoid it. "Why do they have to spin them at face level?" I blurted out, wiping my cheeks. I heard laughter from behind.

Once we dropped in elevation, the hike wasn't crazy long, but it was long enough that if crap hit the fan, it would be quite an ordeal to get help. After wiping the last web off my face—mixed with my sweat, it stuck like glue—the path opened up a bit and jogged left until we reached the wall. Yes, I had been here before, but the enormous wall was so impressive, it stopped me in my tracks. "Wow," I said, gazing upward. I took a swig of water. We were almost there. After a few minutes of hiking with the woods on one side of us and the wall on the other, the trail took a sharp turn to the left, then sloped downward. I paused. From here, I could see the start of the O.R. The stakes were high this morning, and the fresh air seemed laden with something different, something heavier. Maybe it was my own fear I was breathing in and out.

I turned to Chris. He and I had a well-practiced routine before making a climb like this; it involved talking through the risks and the safety, and looking up at the line, pointing fingers towards where we thought we should go. Not today. Instead of talking it over, I quickly and wordlessly changed my shoes, slid my harness on, tied in, and flung the pro over my shoulder. Without another glance backward at Chris, I stepped up on the slab. I was breaking our normal routine, and I was doing it on purpose. I needed something to interrupt my usual pattern of thought and keep my emotions from going where they always did when starting out on a big endeavor—to the bottom of my stomach.

I kept my unusual silence as I climbed. Forty feet up, Chris shouted, "Dude, you're cruising it!" If he wondered why I had broken protocol, he kept it to himself. He stayed focused on being supportive, which I appreciated. I needed to concentrate on sticking every move as I slowly climbed up the featureless slab. With nowhere to set protection, I couldn't afford a single mistake.

As I continued to climb higher, the treetops receded, leaving behind nothing but rock and sun. An endless sea of granite stood between my feet and the summit, but rather than getting overwhelmed, I kept my mind rooted in the moment. So far, the climb was going down as smooth as the first cold beer on a warm summer night. I continued upward; step by step, hand press over hand press, the friction war to the first ledge continued. All of my preparation was paying off in a big way.

Over a hundred feet off the floor, I gained the top of the first pitch. I slung a tree and clipped myself in. "Off belay!" I shouted, elated. I pulled the rope, bringing Chris up to the shrubby ledge. Like me, he was stoked.

"Man, I got to tell ya," Chris said, "I didn't think we were actually going to climb it unless we made it past this pitch."

I'd been thinking the same thing. The unprotected, deadly run-out had been a big concern, but here we stood, pitch number one accomplished. I was grateful that I had changed up our usual routine. The tweak in approach had gotten the result I wanted: It had interrupted my conscious thoughts and fears and sent them packing.

"A tweak in approach can interrupt a normal thought process."

Ladies and gentlemen, I would like to introduce you to the one... the only... the heavyweight champion of the (sales) world:

Pattern interrupt!

Okay, that windup was kind of cheesy, but I'm going with it because it mirrors the excitement of the "aha" moment I had back on the O.R. Thinking about it later, I saw how the principle applied equally well to sales. I've read that in order to change someone's conceptual direction, you must say or do something that disrupts their usual thought process. Sounds complicated, but it makes sense. In a thought process, one idea leads to another like beads on a necklace; the thoughts themselves are distinct from one another, but in a given situation, they follow each other in a preset sequence. If the process is interrupted—if the string holding the necklace together is cut—the preset is broken. Now, a different (and much better) conversation can take place.

Applying this to my sales technique, I saw that I could not change what a customer was thinking, but I could interrupt their pattern of thought. By doing so, I could redirect their line of reasoning.

The old way: Respond to a customer's questions about the truck they're calling about, regurgitating the same specs they probably already know from looking at our website, then listen to them ask for the best price.

The new way: Interrupt the pattern of questions to lead the sales call in a new direction.

On that first pitch of the O.R., I had subtly pivoted away from thoughts about fear and danger by tweaking my usual routine. This opened up the opportunity for a different, more productive mind preset to take over. But what does this look like when I as a sales rep interrupt a customer's preset? In other words, what does this look like in action?

When a customer says something, instead of responding directly, I take an element of whatever was said and build it into an open-ended question, something that has nothing to do with sales. Doing so, I catch the customer off guard—I break the usual pattern and with it the preset.

Here are a few examples.

Customer: "I'm interested in getting a truck."
Me: "Why is that?"

Customer: "I was passing by your lot and saw you had a (fill in the blank)."

Me: "Is that right? Where were you headed?"

Customer: "Do you have warranties on your trucks?"

Me: "We do. I'm curious, why do you ask? Is there something you're concerned about?"

The list of possible examples is endless, but the message is consistent: I want to understand the customer better. Done correctly, it gives the customer two distinct impressions, both effective in a sales situation. First, the customer sees that we're paying close attention to them. This lets them know that we're genuinely interested in them. The second impression builds on the first: Not only are we interested, we're curious to know more.

The best part is that this pattern interrupt differentiates us from the other dealers and sales reps. "Huh?" you may be thinking, "just by asking a question?" Yup. The technique interrupts their initial thinking—"I'll call and get a few specs and a price"—and guides the flow of dialogue in a different direction, nudging the customer out of the groove of their old preset. Our questions lead from one to another, ultimately bringing us to a much better understanding of the customer's world. Even better, now that they're engaged in answering our questions, they're doing all of the talking. We aren't giving out information. We're collecting it.

I finally did it! I figured out the first step to my new sales plan. I put it into practice right away, and as I expected, it was effective. Better yet, it was controllable, repeatable, and trackable. I recorded some of those early sales calls and analyzed how they went. In almost all cases, I could hear a new, unfamiliar tone in the customers' voices—surprise and genuine appreciation for my interest in hearing their story. While it made the customer feel good, it also didn't play into their plan at all. Success!

Core Principles:
- I must begin with the end in mind.
- I must focus on behaviors.
- I must take action because hope is not enough.
- I must take complete ownership.

SALES PLAN:
Interrupt thought pattern and redirect.

THIRTEEN

Make Them Comfortable

– or –

One Down, Nine to Go

STANDING ON OUR LITTLE ledge of the O.R., more than a hundred feet off the deck, Chris and I began restacking our rope and exchanging gear. I unclipped from the tree I'd used as an anchor and gazed to the left. The route wandered twenty feet or so before coming to a bulging flake (like the name implies, a flake is a thin piece of rock that has partially separated or "flaked" off the main wall). Here was our opportunity to make vertical progress.

"This is surreal, dude." I said, shooting a look back to where Chris was still nestled between the rock and a tree. "Hey, looks comfortable," I called out. "I'm jealous!"

He smiled in response.

My left toe smeared on an angled edge and my hands followed. One crossover with my feet led to another as I continued to march towards the flake. Once there, I found a crack to set some gear; with protection taken care of for the moment, I paused. "Man, there really is no end to this thing, is there?" I said, looking up.

Chris laughed. "Nope. Not from here, there's not."

Balancing on a little indentation in the stone, I lifted my right hand, slid it into the flake, then curled my fingers into a fist to keep my hand from slipping out. I was now secure. Up and over that bulge I went, and after gaining the top, the wall tilted back again, making travel easy until I landed on another ledge full of trees and bushes. If I had known it would be the last time I saw vegetation, I might have stayed longer. The sun was bright and strong. I clipped in and pulled rope for Chris. "On belay!"

"Climbing!" His voice floated up from below, and a moment later his head came into view. Like me, he was grinning ear to ear. Oh, we were so happy. Even better, the next pitch looked like a lot of fun! We both plopped on our butts to rest and appreciate our little corner of the world. I felt a sense of accomplishment, but scanning my eyes across the magnificent landscape, I also felt how insignificant I was on this big rock. I was simply a visitor, and before my arrival and after my eventual departure, this enormous sanctuary would remain the same.

"You ready?"

"Yup, onward!"

I slung my rack of gear over my shoulder and faced the wall. Two vertical cracks split the head wall, giving me space in which to jam my hands. "This is gonna be a breeze, dude," I said. With every step and every jam, my smile confirmed my thinking. This was fun. Less than five minutes later, I was clipping into the anchors at the top of pitch three. The sun was gaining strength in the cloudless sky, and I leaned back against an inside shady corner. Instantly recharged, I yelled out, "On belay, bud!" A few minutes later, Chris appeared.

"Nice, dude!" he said as he stepped up onto the ledge. "Man, this next pitch is gonna be a little crazy, huh?"

I was confused. I'd been so focused on getting out of the sun that I hadn't looked up. Now, I saw above us a pitch I had completely forgotten about—almost as though it had been erased from my mental movie altogether. "Oh, my god," I said, shielding my eyes from the sun as I looked upward. The fourth pitch was a pumpy, inside corner thing that traveled upward. Following the line of rock, I could see that we'd be forced to traverse right onto a frighteningly exposed face. The bottom section had a crack splitting the corner—always a welcome sight—but it grew narrower as it climbed and soon disappeared altogether. "This is going to take a bit of effort, physically and mentally," I said, taking a deep breath.

"You got this," Chris replied.

For the first time that day, I wasn't confident that I did. With my gear slung over my shoulder, I turned to face the wall. After a few moments, slowly and awkwardly, I attempted to gain purchase in the crack while pasting my toes against a ripple. My muscles were smoking just trying to hold myself in place. I stepped back down. "Dude, I don't know."

Silence. I knew his silence was meant to give me space to think, but honestly, I could have used a little encouragement. Without a word, I leaned back into the corner and pasted the rubber of my soles hard against the wall while pulling against the inside edge of the crack, giving it every ounce of strength I had. I stuck to it.

"See, you got this!" Chris called from a few feet below.

The corner was not coming easy, and with every move I made, I was over-crimping, over-jamming, and putting a ton more strain on my feet than needed. The sweat was pouring down my face and dripping into my eyes, but I couldn't do anything about it.

"Come on, buddy, you can do it!" That wasn't Chris, by the way. That was me, talking to myself. I reached far to the right to grab a crescent-shaped lip, and a moment later, I powered over the top. Panting and gasping for air, I closed my eyes as I slid onto the ledge and lay facedown on my stomach. "I'm off belay, Chris."

The truth is, if I had climbed this with the same confidence I had the previous pitches, I could have ticked it off in no time. But nope, I had decided to prolong my exposure to hell and turned a forty-foot section into a twenty-minute, all-out brawl against the stone. After several minutes attempting to catch my breath, I sat up with my back against the wall to reset.

I pulled the rope and brought Chris up. He cruised the corner with no issue, proving that the battle had been in my head the whole time. "Man, I feel dumb," I said. "My bad, dude."

Chris grabbed the last hold before reaching the top with his right hand and threw his left towards me to make me stop talking. He climbed up and stood beside me. "This is about as real as it gets," he said. "I absolutely would have done the same thing—or worse!" He turned around to look out, then sank down beside me. "Look at us. And look at this view!"

I expected him to confirm that I was in my head or that I had allowed my fear to take control, but nope, he just wanted me to feel comfortable. Out on the pitch, he could have pushed me when I was floundering. Would it have helped? I doubt it. More likely, it would have turned my entire brain to mush, and I would have rejected anything he said, no matter how much sense it made.

Sitting with our sweaty backs against the stone, both of us knew what was next. A decision. I spoke first. "So, this is the point of no return. Once we start up on this pitch, it's summit or bust."

Chris nodded in agreement. "Yup, absolutely no way to rappel down past this point."

For several moments, he and I admired a flock of birds cruising below us. Chris finally broke the silence. "Seth, I got to say, I hope you know that I'm already super impressed with our day. If you decide you don't want to continue on, you shouldn't feel bad about it. You've killed it already, and I couldn't be happier."

Hearing his words gave me peace, but I knew he wanted to get to the top of the O.R. as much as I did. Still, we were friends, and more than any agenda, he cared about me and how I might be feeling. He knew I had been mentally damaged a bit by the pitch below and wanted to support me. Whatever decision I made, he wanted me to make it without any pressure from him.

"I think I'm in my head a little right now," I admitted.

The second those words exited my mouth, he said, "I totally understand. We can go back down right now."

Filled with appreciation, I turned toward my friend. "Man, am I happy to be in this crapshow of a situation with you, buddy."

"People need to feel okay to have confidence to make a decision."

Being in my head on the O.R. was a tough experience, but reflecting on it later, I realized that you don't have to climb a granite wall to know what stress and uncertainty feel like. When a customer is in the process of making a significant purchase, it can trip off a similar emotional response. While we salespeople are occupied with making the deal, the customer's mind is firing off countless questions: Should I be doing this? Did I think everything over? Is this the right deal for me? The right dealership? What if something goes wrong?

Reader, how in the world do we calm their stress storm? Luckily, we already know the first step: pattern interrupt. This redirection opens up another perspective, a path the conversation can travel down that didn't exist before.

When dialogue gets redirected, walls come down. Instead of, "This is what we've got, do you want it?," we get to listen to our customer and connect on a less transactional level. It's like story-time with the customer. Once we start down that path, it runs out naturally to the end like a river cutting through a canyon.

I'll never forget the first time I experienced this in action. I was at the office and had just sat down at my desk when the phone rang.

"Morning, my name is Eli," an unfamiliar voice said. "I want to know how your financing works."

Remembering to redirect, I responded, "You know, I get that question a lot. Usually it's from someone making the switch from driving for a company to owning their own. Is that you?"

That simple question was all that was needed for Eli to open up! Not only did he answer that question, but he told me everything he'd been thinking about.

"Eli, it sounds like this has been on your brain for quite some time. How long have you been thinking about doing this?"

He didn't hesitate. "Six months."

Just thinking about his long, internal struggle made me exhausted. "Man, that's a long time to think about something. But you called today, so I guess you're confident about doing this, huh?"

He paused a moment. "No, I'm a little nervous."

"What about?" I asked.

I let him pour out his fears without a word of interruption. When he finished, I decided to put his concerns above my own agenda. "I would love to sell you a truck, but there's a lot to think about here, huh?" Eli heard my question loud and clear, although he didn't even acknowledge it. We moved forward. There was nothing I could have said to calm his fears, but after he was comfortable enough to open up, he calmed them himself. That's when it hit me: It's not just about the words spoken, it's about creating a trusting, supportive environment. It's not about the statements made but the questions asked.

Once Eli was comfortable, he was ready to move forward. I wanted to sell a truck as much as he wanted to buy one, but by staying neutral, I let him see that I wanted this to be the right thing for him.

I heard once that customers don't buy when they understand, they buy when they are understood. Agree and amen to that!

Core Principles:
- I must begin with the end in mind.
- I must focus on behaviors.
- I must take action because hope is not enough.
- I must take complete ownership.

SALES PLAN:

Interrupt thought pattern and redirect.

Make them feel okay and comfortable.

FOURTEEN

Actively Listen

– or –

Retreat or Don't Retreat?

CHRIS'S WORDS RANG in my ears: "Dude, we can go back down right now." He was trying to give me some comfort, to reassure me that whatever choice I made was okay with him. As my mind ping-ponged between the two options—keep going or retreat—I caught sight of a blue and yellow tail disappearing into a crack in the wall. The sudden appearance of the lizard on our ledge four hundred feet up gave me some comfort. After a few seconds of silence, I said, "Nope, we're going to do this." By saying the words out loud, I was signing my name to the contract. We were upward bound.

I gathered the pro, and Chris stacked the rope. Dipping my hands in chalk, I let out a long breath. I was still shaky but determined to push forward. The next pitch, the fifth, wasn't the most difficult, but I knew there weren't many places to protect a fall. I had to get my mental game on. I took another deep breath, exhaled, then with my right foot on a little nub, I engaged my core, threw a hand up towards the hold, and…missed it!

"Get a grip, Seth," I mumbled under my breath. I tried again and missed it once more. What the hell was going on with me? This wasn't a particularly difficult move, but I was getting inside my head, the exact opposite of where I needed to be. No more mumbling, now I was chewing myself out audibly. Chris said nothing. My fear was turning into anger—at myself. Still more words of self-criticism poured out of my mouth, with not a word from my buddy. Out of will and rage, I slammed my right foot on the same hold to fire once again. Hey, anger can sure fuel an attempt…I snagged it! Step, hand, step, hand until I reached a decent little edge to balance on.

Now that we had passed the point of no return, I wasn't in my head anymore. The only thing to think about was climbing higher. Another step up, and it was obvious that this next section was going to require me to move delicately. No holds or edges for my hands, just friction for my toes. As my eyes shot forward, my toes dug into the sticky granite, and I stood straight with my palms inches from my chest. I was fifty feet above Chris and fifty feet from the next anchor point. Not quite vertical, but close enough where a slabby, moss-filled section reminded me that if I lost purchase or my weight distribution got out of whack, I would be rewarded with a fast trip to a lower elevation.

In climbing, each foot past protection equals two feet of fall. If I fell now, I would plummet. I concentrated on slowing my racing heartbeat. I was nervous now. I tiptoed my feet gingerly up the rock, my palms pressed upside down against the face of the granite; I was relying entirely on friction. Lucky for me, I'd done this enough times that the movement felt natural. Terrifying, but natural. After about fifteen minutes of this stomach-dropping dance, I was just a few feet from the top of the pitch. Feeling more confident, I snuck a look over my shoulder. I had a panoramic view of the bluest sky and the boldest, most beautiful wall east of the Mississippi; below, the valley was the deepest green I had ever seen. All my fear and anger instantly transformed into joy. I dug my toes into a few more slabby footholds and just like that, without placing any pro, I made it. I set up the anchor underneath a big block, then pulled the rope. "On belay!" I yelled. Within no time, Chris was standing by my side.

"Dude! You didn't place any gear! Holy crap, way to go," he said. My feelings must have been obvious. He took one look at me and immediately yelled with exhilaration. "Wooooo!" The sound descended to the valley below and echoed back up to us.

I looked at my friend. "Hey, man, thanks for listening down there. I just needed to talk through it, I guess."

With that, Chris patted my shoulder. "Anything you need, bud. Just happy to be here."

***

**"A person will usually reveal what is
holding them back if we listen."**

My old goal was to say something that persuaded a customer to move forward with a sale. But with the new perspective gained on pitch five of the O.R., my goal shifted to something new. Now, instead of trying to find the right words to prod the customer forward, I decided I needed to create the environment where the customer did this on their own.

The first step is to get the customer talking. The less I say and the more they talk, the better. Even if what they say seems contrary to what I think will lead to a sale.

Decision made to listen—check! How hard can it be?

As it turns out, harder than I expected. I blame it on an epidemic that's been seen around the globe—what I call "attention-span-of-a-gnat disorder." In a world where technology has sped up every aspect of life, our internal processors—our brains—are taking in more information than ever before. The result is that when we sit down to listen to someone, if what we're hearing is not personally relevant to us, we start to fidget, first internally ("Why is he/she telling me this?"), then, within seconds (at least for me), externally. We wiggle around in our chair, we reposition our arms, we sneak peeks at the clock on the wall. Worst of all, we may even interrupt the speaker. When this happens during a sales conversation, the unintended result is a super-clear message to the customer: "I've heard enough of your thoughts, and I'm not interested unless we're moving forward." Once the customer senses that, why would they ever feel comfortable enough to keep talking?

I needed to assess my ability to listen well to customers. In sales conversations, I started to pay better attention. Was I hanging on the customer's every word? Or was I jumping back to where I wanted the conversation to be? The answer to that question confirmed that my ears needed some cardio workouts.

Listening, even if I got really good at it, wasn't going to be enough. The second step was to stay in the moment and avoid drawing conclusions about the customer and their needs. While judging results is permissible, assuming you know the intentions that lead to those results is a dangerous game. Also, if I'm busy drawing conclusions, I am not completely listening. No, there's only one acceptable conclusion to draw, and it's this: The customer has a good reason for feeling the way they do.

Third step: Seek out opportunities to get the customer talking more. Any open-ended question that encourages them to share more is great. Here's an example:

Customer: "I just don't know if I should be doing this right now."
Me: "You know your situation better than I, why do you feel that way? I want to understand."

The fourth step was the hardest. I had to keep quiet long enough to see if they might just come full circle on a concern without any participation from me. (I know, I know—me keep quiet? Hey, sometimes it happens!)

The gift we give when we listen to our customers is the same gift Chris gave me on the wall: the feeling of being valued, respected, and heard. No matter how silly they (or we) regard their trepidation about making a purchase, we're showing that how they feel and what they want to say is worth listening to. They deserve to make their own decision. We know what we sell and who we are, but without them—each and every customer—we're an equation with a missing piece.

Core Principles:
- I must begin with the end in mind.
- I must focus on behaviors.
- I must take action because hope is not enough.
- I must take complete ownership.

SALES PLAN:
Interrupt thought pattern and redirect.

Make them comfortable.

Actively listen.

FIFTEEN

Let Them Feel Justified

– or –

*It Was Good
Until It Wasn't*

"**I**T'S FREAKING HOT!"

The rays of sun beat down directly overhead. Thank god we were under an overhanging block that offered some shade. As the sweat continued to pour, I carefully grabbed the piece of gear from Chris's hand. Clipped into the belay, I leaned out so I could figure out my next direction of travel. With my eyes panning above and to the sides, I decided to traverse right before moving up and over an overhanging, black jut-out in the wall.

"On belay?"

"On belay, bud!"

I gave a quick nod and with my right hand, I grabbed a small crimp up and onto the black face. Immediately, I knew that this move was going to be bold. My right foot went out, and with a small jump, I grabbed a rounded edge with my left hand.

"Nice work!" Chris yelled from where he stood on belay below.

It was too soon. Just as my second hand slapped the hold, my right foot slipped, leaving me hanging free from my arms hundreds of feet in the air. I could have quickly pasted my foot right back on, but I paused. To be honest, dangling with this kind of exposure was freaking wild. I waited for the surge of adrenaline to abate and for my breathing to slow, then I carefully took a hand off the wall to shake out. After a few seconds, the lactic acid was gone from my forearm, giving me a few more seconds of strength. I reset my foot and powered up to the next hold. Fifteen feet later, I was standing on top of the overhang. "Dude, that was freaking real!" I couldn't see Chris, but I know he had to be feeling it too.

"No doubt, brother!" I heard from below. He was preparing to start this section of the climb, and I could hear the wonder in his voice. "I see why you would feel that. How in the hell did you hold yourself together?"

Shaking my head at his question, I didn't even answer. Honestly, I was already impressed with myself, but to have Chris be impressed too—well, that was even better. I felt empowered.

"That was special, bud," I called out.

I was standing on a ledge three inches wide. To the left a few feet, it doubled in size, so I carefully shuffled over. With both feet secure, I looked up to get a lay of the land. Located straight ahead was a thin seam that snaked its way up for twenty feet before closing up again. With the fingertips of my left hand jammed into that shallow seam for balance, I swiveled to face outward. A flock of birds was circling hundreds of feet below, and the trees were the size of bushes. A few moments wasn't enough time to really appreciate everything, but I had to move on. I hadn't even set any protection yet. A light wind was blowing. Just then, the smallest gust hit me and sent chills down my spine. I turned back to face the wall.

The seam appeared solid enough, but without the sticky rubber of my shoes locking onto a periodic ripple in the stone, I wouldn't make it. This was a feet-smearing (or pressing) thing, but really, it was more of a balancing act. I placed a small cam in the seam and gave it a yank. Pop! It flew right out. My stomach sank. The only spot to place pro, and it wouldn't hold. I tried again and gave it another sharp tug. It wiggled but held. It would have to do.

The first few ripples were big enough for my toes, but the higher I climbed, the smaller they became. Halfway up the seam, a gust of wind caused my center of gravity to tip backwards. I'm not sure if I lost focus or perhaps it was the wind, but I started to lose purchase with my feet, and my fingers almost slid out of the crack.

"OH, SH**!" I cussed, loudly. As I tensed my core and pulled in, I regained my stance. Every muscle in my body was shaking. For the first time, I wasn't just scared; I was terrified. If I had fallen, it would have been game over. I wasn't out of the woods yet, but at least I was leaning in. Quickly, with my stomach still in my throat, I reset my hand and shifted a foot over to a ripple. Just imagining slamming into the block below before falling an additional forty feet had my head spinning. "That was close!" I screamed out.

I had a tough time hearing Chris's reply. "That's totally normal, man. Everyone goes through that. Way to keep with it!"

While he had no idea how close I'd been to disaster, his words filled me with confidence. I cautiously stemmed up another twenty feet until the seam disappeared. Just to the right, I grabbed a horizontal crack and stepped up and over. I grabbed the top and pulled up until my foot was level with my hand. With one big effort, I rocked my body directly over my foot and stood up. I was safely atop the corner.

While I was only a quarter way through pitch six, the rest looked comparatively easy. There was still no place to set any gear, but I could see divots and rounded blobs leading the rest of the way to the anchors. I assumed the position and marched up, swinging my weight back and forth from left to right. Finally, I clipped in. Everything I loved about climbing was currently happening—the movement, the freedom, getting an edge over fear, the wild amount of air. I started pulling up rope and in just a few moments, I had everything reset to bring Chris up.

"On belay, Chris!" I had to shout. The gusts of wind were growing stronger.

A soft muffled noise answered from below. It took awhile before his face popped over the corner, and before he even finished his hand-foot match move to the upper section, he was in full conversation mode. "Epic, brother! You did fantastic! Even on top rope, I'm still shaking."

As he climbed toward me, his words of praise continued. Not going to lie, it made me feel like a million bucks. He clipped into the anchor beside me, turned, and shook his head. "Wow, bud, everything you were saying on that rock? About how hard and terrifying it was? It makes perfect sense. How did you pull through it?" His question didn't really require an answer. But it sure did appeal to my emotions.

**"Everyone loves to feel justified,
even if what they're saying is not."**

Reader, if you believed something to be true and I implied it wasn't, would that change your mind? How do you feel when someone tells you that you're wrong? Of course, people sometimes are wrong. And when that "people" is your customer, it's especially difficult not to jump in and correct them.

Reader: "But isn't that part of our job? To help them understand the truth?"

Me: Nope, reader, it's not.

We need to create the environment for the customer to decide the truth. At first, it doesn't matter what is true, it only matters what they believe it to be. Their statements, expectations, and reasons might not make sense to us, but they do to them. What we as salespeople need to know is why they feel the way they do, and what led them down that path in the first place. Once we know this, a discussion is possible, but only if they aren't feeling like they're under attack. I'd like to share some examples of how to do that:

Replying to a customer the wrong way:
"Seriously? You think that?"
"I don't know where you heard that, but it's wrong."
"What you said doesn't make much sense."

Replying to a customer the right way:
"I never thought about it that way."
"What a great point."
"A lot of people feel that way."

After assuring the customer we're hearing what they're saying, we follow up with a question:

"So that we're on the same page, can you walk me through how you got there?"
"Can you share why you feel that way?"
"I would love to learn, can you teach me how you came up with that?"

Again, the purpose of this is to make customers feel confident and at ease, not to sell our product. The more the communication focuses on the customers, their reasoning, and their situation, the more justified they feel and the more comfortable they are.

Core Principles:

- I must begin with the end in mind.
- I must focus on behaviors.
- I must take action because hope is not enough.
- I must take complete ownership.

SALES PLAN:

Interrupt thought pattern and redirect.

Make the customer comfortable.

Actively listen.

Let them feel justified.

SIXTEEN

Set Expectations and Shift Control

– or –

A Conversation from the Ledge

WE HAD TOPPED THE sixth pitch of the O.R., and I was feeling more empowered than I had the entire day. I was eager to push on.

It's an unfortunate circumstance of climbing that a surge of confidence quickly gives way to concern about the next pitch. In this case, the next one was the "crux," the most difficult of the entire climb. As Chris gulped from his water bottle, I focused my attention on the gigantic wall. This was going to challenge every muscle in my body, including the one inside my head.

Chris clipped his bottle onto his harness and joined me in gazing up at the next couple hundred feet of stone. "This is going to be interesting," he said.

Around knee high, the wall leaned out at a forty-five-degree angle for about five feet before turning back in. That doesn't sound too hard, but when you add in that the overhang is polished smooth and the slant inward has nothing to offer by way of purchase, it changes the game.

To add to the challenge, after ten feet, there was nowhere to place any pro, period. Neither of us could see the end of the pitch, but I recalled from our previous climb a hole high above. The wind was whipping hard. Standing just feet away from each other on our foot-wide ledge in the sky, we had to yell to be heard. "Dude, imagine how it's going to be once I turn over this lip. We'll be traveling blind," I said.

Chris turned towards me, his red hair flapping in the wind. "We can't afford for anything to go wrong here. Not on this section."

I couldn't have agreed more. "Okay, when I give the rope a yank twice, that will be your cue to take me off belay. And when you see we have only fifteen feet of rope left, I need you to yank three times. Cool?"

He repeated what I had said to confirm.

"Also, we need a plan in case I reach a point where I have to down-climb. What should I do to signal you to start pulling rope back in?"

Smart guy, Chris is. Both of us had enough experience this high up to know that hearing someone yelling isn't the problem—understanding what they're saying is. He thought about it for maybe two seconds. "Easy. Stay quiet until you need to down-climb and at that point, yell."

Because the stakes were so high and there was absolutely zero room for error, we repeated our plan to each other another two times. We not only knew what each of us was responsible for, but we understood what the other was expected to do as well.

Neither of us minded the repetition a bit. Most accidents on multi-pitch walls are simply the result of a breakdown in communication. When fatigue mixes with fear, just a smidge of that miscommunication can spell disaster quickly. With so many unknowns, confidence in each other's actions was the only thing we could be certain of. Chris was holding the rope—and literally, my life—in his hands.

**"People want to know what to expect. It's fair to the customer
and sales rep both to make expectations clear."**

Without clearly establishing what each of us had to do before
undertaking the crux pitch, Chris and I would have been risking
our lives (even more than we already were). Skip this step in a sales
conversation, and you risk killing the deal.

By following the steps I've already covered, I knew I was laying
the groundwork for a conversation in which the customer would
feel in control. But I also knew that on its own, that wasn't enough.
The customer needed to know what to expect so they could decide
if they were ready, willing, and able to buy. On the flip side, I needed
to know if they could buy what I sold. Setting expectations ensures
that both parties' needs are met.

Applying my new knowledge, I learned that making the transition from a friendly, casual, question-filled conversation to setting
expectations can be awkward. But get it right, and it shifts control.
Get it wrong—which happened plenty of times when I started using the technique—and it triggers the alarm on the customer's internal warning system. Once that alarm sounds in their head, walls
go up, and open dialogue stops.

It took some practice, but I figured out how to make this transition smooth. Let me demonstrate:

Me: "Thanks for sharing your story. Just so I know, what are you
hoping to accomplish today? I want to know if I can help."
Customer: "I want to see what trucks you have and if I like your
financing."
Me: "Perfect. How much time do you have to do that?"
Customer: "Two hours."
Me: "That can happen. I imagine that you have a ton of questions

for me and truthfully, I have some questions for you, too. I don't want to waste your time or mine. We might decide that we aren't a fit for each other and that is more than okay. If I see that we can't help you, I will tell you. I hope that if you don't feel comfortable, you will do the same. Is that fair?"

Customer: "Yes."
Me: "Cool. If neither of us says anything, I will assume that we are moving forward and we can decide what the next steps are."
Customer: Nods their head—and usually gives a sigh of relief.

Let's break it down, reader. By following the pattern above, I accomplish my objective of setting expectations. *This is what you, the customer, can expect from me, and this is what I, your sales rep, can expect from you.* To be successful, I have to be clear about what those expectations are. Typically they revolve around the amount of time the customer has, questions I need to answer for the customer, my own agenda regarding the potential sale, and the customer's commitment to making a decision. (On a side note: A decision does not necessarily mean closing a sale; it means agreeing specifically to the next step.) Yep, it really is that easy. By keeping it clear and simple, we're priming the customer for what's to come. I'd like to share a story about the first time I employed this technique.

One morning a customer named Justin called. Justin had an opportunity to make a ton of money, but to do so he would need his own truck. He told me he might come in the next day. Reader, notice anything about that previous statement? Yep, he said he might come in. That's not a commitment, but I could turn it into one.

"Perfect," I said. "And just so we're on the same page, what are you looking to accomplish tomorrow?" (Notice what I did? I turned possibly tomorrow into a definitely tomorrow.)

Justin said that aside from wanting to see the truck in person, he was interested in doing a credit application.

"We should be able to do that. How much time will you have to get that done?"

"A couple of hours."

"That can work. Hey, if everything sounds good to you at the end, what do you see happening? Will you be looking to commit to the truck or is there anything else?"

He said as long as he liked the truck and the credit app got approved, he would be ready to make the purchase.

This was my opportunity to NOT do what I had always done in the past, which would have been some version of "Great, see you tomorrow. Looking forward to it!" Instead, I set expectations by responding, "Awesome. I'll have the truck pulled up for you. For the credit app, aside from your personal information, they'll also need to verify your employment history and your new haul source. What time should I have that truck up front for you?"

"Noon."

I could not believe it. He actually had given me a firm time. My plan had worked! "I have it inked in. Looking forward to meeting you tomorrow at twelve."

The next day when Justin came in at noon, the truck was parked up front. He looked it over then climbed in to take it for a test drive.

"I take it that you're happy with the truck?" I asked when he got back.

He smiled and nodded as we walked inside. After he completed the credit app, we got word that he was approved. "Great. I'll think everything over tonight and get back with you tomorrow," he said.

What!!?

"Justin, I'm confused. Yesterday you said that if you liked the truck and you got approved for financing, you were ready to commit. You got the financing, so it must be something else. What's making you uncomfortable?"

I could see in his eyes that he remembered what he had committed to. This conversation would have never happened if he had not agreed to make a decision about the truck that day. In essence, his earlier verbal commitment had created a new situation, one that wouldn't have existed had I not made the effort to set clear expectations for both of us.

This was in contrast to my old way of doing things: Justin walks away to "think about it," and I'm left with no other option but to smile and say, "Sure, go ahead. And remember I still really, really want to work with you." (Yeah, I know, I also could have asked, "What do you have to think about?" but that question has lost its punch after being used and abused for decades.)

Justin told me that now that he had the approval, he realized how many other things he needed to get lined up, and it was making him feel overwhelmed. It was time for me to adapt. Because of his honesty (and because of my setup and question), we were able to back it up, and I started helping him get everything else together. Once some of those things were addressed, he was comfortable committing. In the end, he purchased the truck. It didn't happen right away, but it wouldn't have happened at all had I not set expectations that first day.

Before I learned to make this step part of every sales conversation, I'd had far too many customers take up my entire day, only to thank me for my unpaid time with, "I need to think about it." But was this the customer's fault? No. I was responsible.

No more of that. Sales stakes are high, and I have zero interest in being an unpaid consultant. If the customer expects me to work for them, I expect the same level of commitment in return. It's only fair. If they don't commit to making a decision one way or the other, I pass. A decision to not make a decision, is a decision. NEXT!

Core Principles:

- I must begin with the end in mind.
- I must focus on behaviors.
- I must take action because hope is not enough.
- I must take complete ownership.

SALES PLAN:

Interrupt thought pattern and redirect.

Make them comfortable.

Actively listen.

Let them feel justified.

Set expectations to shift control.

Interlude:

A Brief Description
of Two Climbing Moves

In climbing, there are two types of movement: static and dynamic. Static movements are controlled, pre-calculated, and don't rely on momentum to climb upward. These account for the majority of the moves on a climb. In fact, if you have ever climbed a rock wall at a fair or a gym, static movement is what you did the entire time. Move a foot, move a hand, step, and repeat.

Dynamic movements, on the other hand, take equal measures of power, momentum, technique, and courage. To picture it, imagine that your next hand hold is out of reach. Your only option is to turn into a human pendulum: Shifting your weight over your hips, you swing your body as you let go of the rock completely, pushing yourself off as hard as you can. Airborne and fighting gravity, you grab the next hold, which is hopefully now within reach. You want to hit the hold at the apex of your jump because if you don't, your weight will shock-load your hand, and you will fly off. Words fail to describe how much you don't want that to happen.

The biggest difference between dynamic and static moves is that usually, you can reverse a static move by down-climbing. Dynamic moves, however, are nearly always irreversible; if something doesn't go right, you get some air-time, and Newton's law of gravity is re-affirmed. Pulling off a dynamic move is by far the more rewarding of the two, but in order to get that reward, you must be willing to forfeit your sense of safety.

SEVENTEEN

Seek Out the Why

– or –

Why Do We Do This?

"MY WATER IS ALMOST GONE." Chris was looking through the clear plastic of his water bottle.

I glanced at my own. "I'm good. Sixteen ounces left." The sun was at its hottest, and I could feel fatigue slowly starting to set in. Leaning back in my harness, I tore open an energy bar while planning my next sequence of moves.

"Why do we love doing this so much?" Chris asked jokingly. He was restacking the rope for our next pitch, and a steady stream of sweat was dripping off the tip of his nose to the rock at his feet. "I'm literally melting right now. This is our idea of a good time? What the hell is wrong with us?" he said with a laugh.

"Guess we like the abuse," I responded. "On belay, bud? Pitch number seven!" I was ready.

Chris sat back in his harness to get comfortable. "Climb on, brother!"

As my body shifted left from the anchors, I bent backwards to offset the overhang of the wall and gingerly shuffled my feet. I was breathing slowly. I had to. One ounce of an uncontrolled shift in weight on this stretch would send me hurtling downward. There was nothing on the wall to grab except a little crease. I ran my hand over it and laughed. "This isn't even a crease, just a tiny indentation."

Chris looked up and started chuckling. "What the hell, is that supposed to be a hold?"

I pressed my hand sideways into the groove and shot my right toe up to about hip level. This was going to take one bold dynamic move. With every ounce of strength I had, I rocked, swiveled, and fired. Just as my foot cut loose, my left hand aimed for a rounded-off blob high above. Slap! I nailed it. Grunting and straining, I attempt to regain control of all hundred and sixty pounds of my body. With my feet flapping in the air and my muscles screaming, I held my breath and flung my right arm up and onto a divot.

"What a move!" Chris yelled as my feet landed on a piece of granite crystal.

I felt buoyant at having pulled off the audacious move. Grinning from ear to ear, I tiptoed up a few feet to find a secure stance. After looking up at the next hundred feet of unprotected travel ahead, I hollered, "Hell, yeah, Chris, this is why we do it!"

With a big smile, Chris shot his arm victoriously in the air. "Woo hoo!"

"Discovering a customer's why is the most important piece."

Most of us have probably heard the phrase, "If you have a customer willing and able, you have a sale." I don't disagree. But it's insane how we focus on only one part of that equation, the "able." I get it—we don't want to spend our time with someone who can't buy. But even more painful than spending time with someone who can't buy is to spend time with someone who can buy but won't. The "why" is the catalyst and driving force behind each decision made.

It's the influencer that forces one to take action. Without it, our product doesn't matter.

How do we get to the customer's why? After setting expectations, we throw in a pattern interrupt. The customer expects us to talk about finances, but instead, we return to the previous topic, the one they were already comfortable talking about: them.

Here's an example to illustrate:

Jack came by our lot on Friday afternoon. "My company is forcing me to stay out for weeks at a time," he said. "If I get my own truck, I can come home more often."

While that sounded like a good enough reason to me, I sensed it was just the surface. I began, as usual, by setting expectations, then continued by trying to figure out his "why." We chatted for a few more minutes, and then I said, "I didn't ask then, but Jack, I'm curious—can you tell me more about your company keeping you out for long stretches at a time? I want to understand what you're going through."

BOOM! He erupted in emotions as he told me how his one-year-old baby didn't even recognize him and how his wife was fed up with parenting alone. Sticking to my new sales technique, I listened. It wasn't even just technique: I truly wanted to hear what he had to say so I could help him. When he finished, I asked, "Have you told your company about this?"

Jack nodded. "But they won't do anything about it." No longer was Jack buying a truck, Jack was trying to keep his family together. (I could relate to that!) It wasn't simply the price of my truck that Jack had to consider, but the price of being with his family.

Scratching the surface of someone's "why" is not enough. Our willingness and ability to dive deeper by asking more questions strengthens our position. Some might say this is being too intrusive, but I see it from a different angle. Showing an interest in the personal issues that drive our customer's actions is a mark of compassion.

How can we hear about a customer's problem or challenge and not be curious? Even worse, how can we listen and then immediately dismiss their problems and switch gears to what is important to us?

Reader, if you had a friend who told you his wife had left him, would you respond with "Great! Thanks for telling me. Now, what kind of wife would you like to replace her with?" Of course not! More than likely, you'd respond with questions that showed your concern. "Oh my god, what happened? And when was this? Are you okay? Do your kids know? What are you going to do?" All in the most empathetic tone possible.

To put it in terms of selling a truck, imagine this conversation:

Customer: "I had a couple trucks go down last night, and I need replacements."

Me: "Oh man, what happened? Are your drivers okay? Did you have to rescue the loads? I can only imagine that you had a frustrating morning making calls. How much time has that cost you? How did your haul source take the news? Are they working with you? You said ASAP, what does that mean exactly? What will happen if you don't get them replaced by then? Will you lose the haul source completely or just the lost revenue of the loads? Lost revenue—how many loads a day do your trucks handle? That is a lot! I can see why this is so important."

Naturally, you don't want to throw all the questions out at once, but these should give you an idea of how to empathize with your customer's situation and at the same time recognize their "why."

What I've been describing is at odds with our usual way of conducting sales. The traditional way starts with the products we have available and ends with the customer asking for the best price. We remain clueless to the severity of their need. This new path leads to a clear picture of the customer's "why," taking the main focus off the price. Not only do most customers keep talking, they partially close the sale themselves!

The upshot is that customers buy for their reasons, not ours. Having a discussion about their "why" nudges them to consider what is important and prompts them to answer the question, what is this worth to me? Momentum gained!

Core Principles:

- I must begin with the end in mind.
- I must focus on behaviors.
- I must take action because hope is not enough.
- I must take complete ownership.

SALES PLAN:

Interrupt thought pattern and redirect.

Make them comfortable.

Actively listen.

Let them feel justified.

Set expectations.

Seek out the why.

EIGHTEEN

Discuss Money on Our Terms

– or –

A Sea of Hell

THE SEEMINGLY NEVER-ENDING, featureless wall looming ahead made me nervous. My heart rate, which had spiked on the overhang I'd just climbed, was still racing. As I zeroed in on the gray slab above, it was obvious: This was going to be an insecure, friction-dependent crawl. "This will probably be the last time we can talk," I said to Chris.

He nodded. "Got it, I'm with ya, bud." I waited a few more seconds for him to pull in the few inches of slack in the rope before turning back.

"Here we go," I whispered as my trembling right foot dug in. This section reminded me of the first pitch, which now seemed like an eternity ago. Now I was exhausted and soaked with sweat. "It's the same moves, just a little higher," I told myself. I looked down one last time at the seven hundred feet of air below me. "Okay, maybe a lot higher."

I pressed my fingertips against the wall and dropped my gaze to look for my next foot placement. There was nothing. The only way to gain elevation would be to locate and execute friction points. As

I slowly lifted a foot, my rubber sole dug into a small crystal, and I weighted it. It stuck. I repeated the move with the other foot. With deep, controlled breaths, I duplicated the move, first with one foot and then the other, over and over. It was slow going, but it was working. "Okay, this will go. Steady, bud," I muttered hesitantly. For the next twenty minutes, I crawled up inch by inch until I finally stepped up to a decent stance. I paused and looked down. Perhaps I shouldn't have. My eyes followed the dangling orange rope down the wall until it was out of sight. Feeling uneasy, I shook my head. Then I caught a glimpse of something on the rock that made my stomach drop: water.

Water, as I've said, is the enemy of friction, and friction was the only thing keeping me glued to the face of the wall. I forgot to breathe as I stepped up to scan the rock. There was no avoiding it; every route upward glistened with rivulets of water. I moved my left foot carefully onto the slippery stone. My breaths came in little gasps. Looking at my hands, which were now soaking wet, I knew that I was going to have to get a grip on my fear if I wanted to continue. And continuing was the only option I had.

This hellish spot on the wall was going to be home until I decided to move past it. I was eighty feet past my protection, and increasing the distance was not ideal, but the pain of staying was more costly. "Seth, you gotta breathe and go," I told myself. I took my own advice. Step over step, palm press over palm press, I traveled until I caught sight of the large hole I had remembered from my earlier climb, up and to the left. My pace quickened. "I'm going make it!" The very second my hand reached the ledge, all of my fear vanished. My palms pushed against the edge of the opening, and I heaved myself up and over.

For the next several moments, I sat in the comfort of my shady cave, repeatedly wiping the sweat from my forehead. In an attempt to slow my heart rate, I closed my eyes and listened to the breeze that blew across the opening of the cave. "Oh, crap!" My eyes shot open. "Chris is probably burning alive down there!" The security and comfort of being tucked inside a nook of the wall had caused a temporary memory lapse; Chris and I might have been connected by rope, but it was as if we were on two different planets. Quickly, I set up the belay, about six feet from the edge. After pulling in just four arm-lengths of rope, it went taut—I had almost run out of rope! "On belay!" I yelled. When I leaned out, all I could hear was the wind smacking the face of the wall. I gave the rope a couple of hard yanks and waited. Within a few seconds, my hand felt the force of the rope being stretched. I smiled. Chris was climbing.

As I slowly pulled in slack, I couldn't help but admire my surroundings. The cave was an almost perfect six-by-six cube and from where I stood, the floor, ceiling, and side walls resembled the frame of a picture. *This is so pretty*, I thought. I pulled rope for quite some time until Chris's unmistakable red hair popped into sight.

"Dude, I almost puked when I saw the water."

I laughed. "Yeah, that was real."

He clipped into the anchors and turned out to face the opening. "Wow. Want to hang out here for a bit?"

We scooted our butts to the edge so that our legs dangled free. Looking down, I could still see birds flying in circles, but now they weren't much more than black dots in the sky. "It really isn't about the size of the wall or even the difficulty," I said. "It's about our position on it that matters most, huh?"

Chris bobbed his head in agreement. "Totally, dude. I mean, look at the ground! From up here, you can't even make out the trees."

He wasn't wrong. The valley below was enormous, its details softened and blurred. I shifted my attention back to the wall. About two hundred feet to our right, a massive pinnacle leaned up against the main wall, looking like it could topple over at any second. It started from the ground and rose all the way to the top. I did a double take. "Oh, my god, Chris, I can see the top!" I felt a new surge of motivation.

Chris must have felt the same. "Only three pitches left, Seth!" He reached over and we slapped hands.

"The size of the wall doesn't matter, it's where we're on it that does!" I said.

With a wry smile, Chris stood up and held his right hand out like he was holding a glass for a toast. "To where we're at."

I raised my imaginary glass with a quick nod. "To where we're at."

**"Meet our customers where they're at,
but discuss money on our terms."**

What does it cost?

Setting a price is a major part of every sale. Price is top-of-mind for most customers, and getting it right is one of the biggest hurdles a sales rep must jump in order to close the deal. We don't want to lose deals based on price, but we don't want to win them solely based on price, either. This step, more than any other, depends less on the exact words spoken than it does following the correct thought process. Remember, it's not the price of the truck but rather our position while discussing it that makes the sale.

 First, it's important to remember what is in the mind of the customer. In most scenarios, they've already spent time swiping right on their phone to find the cheapest price for the item they want. They chose to call the place that had the best price to see if they could get that price even lower. If they saw what they want listed for $33,000, they believe $30,000 is what they should pay. If the price is $45,000, they'll try to get it for $40,000—for no other reason than that's what past dealings have taught them to expect. Reader, tell me that we don't do the same thing! It's an old model of negotiation passed down through the generations. And with the customers' mental maps directing their focus to buy based on best price, it should be no shock that price comes up quickly on every call. It is for that reason that redirecting the call from the beginning is so important.

If we've followed the previous steps, we've already discussed the reasons they're buying and what pain the purchase will alleviate. We, and they, are clear on their "why." This conversation will have compelled them to consider the price of their situation, not just the price of the truck. This is great news, because we need to now figure out if they are able to buy. With their preset mental maps reconfigured, we can change the order of conversation, thus yielding a wildly different result.

The old way:

Customer opens negotiation: "You said your price was $53K, would you take $50K?" This forces us into a defensive position.

The new way:

We open the negotiation not with a number but with a question: "I see now why buying a truck is so important to you. I'm curious, what amount would you be comfortable spending?" After they state an amount, we follow with, "And what exactly were you expecting to get for that?"

When we subvert the order of the conversation in this way, we no longer have to defend ourselves against a customer's opening salvo. Instead, it's up to the customer to open with a price and the reason they're willing to pay it. The more detailed their explanation, the better. After they paint a clear picture of what they want, we can respond in one of two ways.

1) Meet them at or under their budget: "Great news! I have what you want, and it's priced under what you hoped to spend. Here, let me show you."

2) If we don't have exactly what they want or if the item is over their budget: "Thank you for sharing. I want to be respectful of your time. From what you just said, we might have hit a wall. For the budget you described, we don't have that exact truck. (Brief pause.) I hate to ask, but does this mean that we should stop?"

But the second option is risky, you might be thinking. And I would agree if the right tone, approach, and genuine concern were not present from the beginning. It's important that the customer knows we care about what's good for them. Demonstrating this from the outset builds their faith and trust in us. When we have that, there's little risk that they will want to stop the sales conversation—even if that's exactly what we suggest doing.

It's a potent tactic. We haven't given any information on pricing, yet we're implying that we're ready to walk away from the sales conversation. What makes this work? The deployment of two psychological weapons.

First, the scarcity rule. It's the one used by sales reps when they say, "You better get in here quick before someone else buys it!" The one that makes me most hungry for Chick-fil-A on Sundays, when they're closed, or makes my kids ignore a toy until someone else picks it up and walks off to play with it. Sure, it's real, but in addition to the fact that our customers hear this coming from a mile away, it's been so overused that it's no longer believable. Then why are we discussing it? Because when we reconfigure the equation, it's just as powerful as ever. Instead of making the *product* scarce, we're insinuating that we're about to make *ourselves* scarce.

The second weapon is the non-explained "why." We've been conditioned since childhood not to accept any statement without understanding the reason behind it. The sales rep's move to end the conversation, startling and surprising to the customer, triggers a predictable human response: the need to know why. The internal crapfest between their ears won't let them end the conversation without getting answers, and that's when the leverage shifts in our favor. "What do you have? Where do I need to be flexible?" the customer will ask. We now hold the advantage.

Core Principles:

I must begin with the end in mind.

I must focus on behaviors.

I must take action because hope is not enough.

I must take complete ownership.

SALES PLAN:

Interrupt thought pattern and redirect.

Make them comfortable.

Actively listen.

Let them feel justified.

Set expectations.

Seek out the why.

Discuss money on our terms.

NINETEEN

Merge Process and Expectation

– or –

Twenty Minutes of Courage

"IT'S COMICAL HOW QUICKLY life can change," Chris said with only a touch of irony.

As I leaned over to start stacking rope, I couldn't help but agree. Just moments before, we were laughing as our legs dangled carelessly, but now, gazing at the dark gray polished granite above, I felt my stomach churn. For the next eighty feet, the upper headwall of the O.R. swooped inward, then outward. It had the concave shape of a skateboarder's halfpipe and was just as smooth. My hands started to sweat as I ran my fingers over the glassy rock. I took a deep breath. "Chris, if I blow this, it's gonna suck." Just imagining the injury from sliding and bouncing off the rock had me terrified.

Chris nodded. He pointed to a spot about forty feet over. "Looks like a crack to set gear, if you can make it that far."

I saw it, but doubts were scrabbling to get purchase in my mind. "I don't know if I can do it, dude." Here is the truth, reader. The stretch of wall ahead wasn't something you just have a go at. "Hoping for the best" was not an option. I am beyond grateful that life gives us many situations to try and fail, but our eighth pitch was not one of them. The only option was to succeed. "I guess we can't stay here," I said, looking back at our comfy cave.

Chris put me on belay, and as I scooted out to the ledge, he offered some words to motivate me. "Just remember that while you're freaked out and sweating to death, I will be…safe in my shady cave." He grinned.

"Shut up, Chris!" With a smile, I moved my left toe over, shut my eyes, and took a long, deep breath in. "I have to get my heart rate down to pull this off, bud. And by the way, you're a butthole." Chris's laughter filled the air as I began to move. My left toe dug in, the right followed suit, and my core tensed as I crimped one micro-edge after another. Slowly and steadily, I placed my extremities on the wall with precision. Every move needed to be flawless.

I came to a sudden standstill. In a panic, my eyes darted to locate the next ripple, divot, or crystal. Nothing. As I stepped up insecurely, my attention wandered to the void below. "No!" I said aloud, shaking my head. My focus had to remain on what was holding me to the wall. With my two middle fingers pressed against a divot, I crossed over with my feet and released my hand. I was balancing on two quarter-inch crystals and nothing else. As I slowly dropped my arms behind my back to powder up my sweaty hands, I spotted the crack. Just twenty minutes ago, it had seemed like a mile away, but now it was almost within arm's reach.

"I got this!" I called out half nervously, half excitedly, as I placed protection into the most perfect crack I could hope for.

"This route is living up to our expectations, brother!" he hollered back.

I jammed another cam to double up on pro and locked my fingers in it. "Yup, expectations met. This is wild." The crack fizzled out a short way up, but as it did, the wall kicked back a touch, making the next fifty feet of travel enjoyable. As I tiptoed up the last few inches leading to the anchors, I stopped to look around. I was on top of the world. With the O.R. in front of me and the jagged shadows of the southern Blue Ridge mountains to my side, I felt wonderful. Clipping in, I howled like a wolf under a full moon. Back under the hot rays of the sun, I hurried to bring Chris up. As he neared the anchor where I stood, he mimicked my howl. "Woo! Only two more pitches to go!"

***

"Their expectations are just as important as our process."

Before we dive into this last step of qualifying a buyer, I have a story. My youngest daughter and I were playing outside one day when she suddenly lined up next to me, crouched down, and shifted her weight onto her left foot. She locked eyes with me and gave me a grin. I laughed. My daughter wanted to compete with me in a footrace! Looking straight ahead, I counted down from three and took off like a shot. Race on! I smoked her, but when I turned around, she was still standing where we had started. Confused, I asked her, "Why didn't you run?"

She looked almost ashamed. "I didn't know we were racing."

Isn't that just like sales? We run forward believing all is well, only to turn back to see the customer standing in the same spot. Making assumptions can be deadly for a sales deal.

One morning at work, a young guy in his mid-twenties walked in. His name was Rick, and he had landed a new opportunity to make a ton of money hauling for the army, but he needed a truck to do it. We discussed the budget and all was well. *Slam freaking dunk*, I thought.

"Hey, since you're ready, I just need you to sign here and wire the money," I said, placing the contract in front of him. When I looked up, I saw that Rick's demeanor had changed. He looked freaked out. "I thought you were good to go, but I can tell that my assumption was wrong. Is there something I missed?" I said.

The truth came out of Rick pretty quickly. "I'm not mechanically inclined, and I don't really know how to make sure everything is okay. My brother works on trucks, and I wanted him to check it out first. I thought I could do that before buying."

Whoops! It wasn't enough to just know Rick's "why" and his budget. I had mistakenly assumed Rick was ready to close the deal, and I was wrong. I needed to know Rick's expectations of the sales process.

We deserve to know the customer's expectations as much as they deserve to know our process. Sometimes, our experience locks us into a mental prison, causing us to follow our processes blindly. Unfortunately, this sometimes leaves customers on the outside—locked out of understanding our process—which reduces our ability to accommodate them. Only when we know what they expect can we meet them where they are. Then, and only then, is there a chance to effectively merge our process and their expectations. This question, asked early on, can give us incredible insight into their world: "I'd like to know what you need in order to feel comfortable making this decision. Would you mind walking me through it? I want to make sure that I can do it."

The information we seek about the sale includes:
• the timing
• who is involved
• where it needs to happen
• how it needs to happen

If there's more to their story, we can follow up with further questions. By minimizing false assumptions and making room for clients' expectations, we create an environment in which sales go up and the amount of time spent per transaction goes down.

Core Principles:
- I must begin with the end in mind.
- I must focus on behaviors.
- I must take action because hope is not enough.
- I must take complete ownership.

SALES PLAN:

Interrupt thought pattern and redirect.

Make them comfortable.

Actively listen.

Let them feel justified.

Set expectations.

Seek out the why.

Discuss money on our terms.

Merge process and expectation.

TWENTY

Build Confidence

– or –

Tripod in the Sky

"**I**S THAT A PLANT?" Chris asked, pointing toward a ledge high above. He squinted with his left hand pressed against his forehead, shielding his eyes from the strong afternoon sun, then laughed with excitement. "Seth, it is!"

As I shoveled the rope on top of itself to reset, I couldn't help but smile. Seeing vegetation meant that we were close to the top. Really close. I stood to catch a glimpse of the next section of wall. Steep. I leaned in to press my face against the wall and saw that it kicked out a bit. The sun reflected off the light gray stone as if the wall were a mirror. Little holes and pockets littered this next section of wall, and I couldn't help but feel a little relieved. Judging by their size, there was a chance they'd be the best holds on the entire route.

"Wonder why that's there?" Chris asked, pointing to a bolt about twenty feet up. I shrugged and thought, *a bolt, even better.* We shot each other a quick smile. This wasn't going to be so rough after all.

"Climb on, Seth!" Chris yelled, as if I wasn't standing a foot away. We both chuckled. We were feeling pretty optimistic.

The mood didn't last long. The second my right hand made contact with the first pocket and before my foot even left the ground, it was apparent that the steep slant of the pitch neutralized whatever advantage the divots and holes provided. They did not offer security, and the poor friction made it clear why someone had taken the time to place a bolt. Planted on the wall, I resorted to performing a hip, core, and forearm game. Basically, I twisted myself into a human tripod in the sky. Switching feet for balance, throwing a leg out wide to offset weight, and swiveling hips to keep my body sucked into the wall, I began to enjoy the flow of movement. After about ten feet of elevation gain, I dropped my glance downward. "Wow!" I gasped. Hundreds of feet of air separated me from solid ground. Before I could take it all in, I was reminded that I was currently climbing on borrowed time. My forearms were starting to smoke as the lactic acid set in with a vengeance. Hanging from my fingers, I shook out one arm at a time. I had to move quickly if I didn't want the open air to be my next destination.

"Keep moving, Seth!" Chris yelled as I swung for the next hold. I fired up again and dug my right toe into a hole. The shiny bolt was just four feet away. "I got this," I whispered to myself. As soon as the words exited my mouth, I shot up again. One more move! I couldn't locate my next hold. I whipped my head left to right in a panic. My arms were on fire, and as my internal time bomb ticked away, I was stopped dead in my tracks. Up and to the left, an indentation marking the top of the steep part of the wall caught my eye. With only seconds of strength left, I swung out in a desperate move to lock onto the small edge. I made it. I clipped the bolt and mantled over.

"Nice!" I heard Chris say from below.

Now that I was over the steep section, I leaned into the wall. Sweat was pouring, and I was exhausted. It felt like an eternity as I tried to control my racing pulse, but for the next few moments, I stood on my inch-wide, sloping indentation with eyes shut, trying to regain control of my breathing. "I'm not out of the woods yet!" I called back to Chris. Now that I was clipped onto the bolt, my headspace was much better. With my palms pressed against the upper section of the pitch, I pushed out from the wall to examine what came next. After just a step or two, the wall leaned in. With my forearms relieved, the climbing was back to my toes, and my confidence was restored. As I continued upward, little moss pads growing from the rock began to appear, and I saw trees on the ledge above. I ducked underneath a low-hanging branch to finish up this formidable ninth section and felt a surge of pure joy. Wrapping a sling around a branch to tie in, I hollered, "Off belay!"

**"Closing a sale requires confidence—
on the part of the sales rep *and* the customer."**

"Your price is too high." It's the sentence we've all heard a million times. Until we get past it, there's no closing the sale. At this point, plenty of the sales gurus with their objective-solving responses will be itching to use the same closes they've fired off for years—the same closes customers have heard a million times before. The only effect these well-worn statements have is to signal to the customer that they're being sold. But customers don't want to be sold, they want to be helped.

An odd thing I've noticed is that as sales reps, we feel wonderful firing off a close. But my thinking is that if a "close" makes us feel great, it probably has the opposite effect on our customer.

The magic of following this new strategy is that for the most part, we've already discovered the customer's objections and have overcome them one at a time. Customers still want the best price and inevitably, they will ask for it. The secret is to say no to their request without killing their confidence—and with it their ability to commit to a decision. Remember, it's not what we say, but what we ask.

"Your prices are high."

I'd been talking to the customer for a while about a truck he was interested in. Hearing the tired old line about prices being high didn't stop me; the trick now was to respond in a way he didn't expect. "Believe it or not, I've heard that before," I said. "But tell me, what makes you think so?"

"I saw a similar truck at one of your competitors listed for less."

"Makes sense. Does that mean you would rather work with them?"

He froze for a moment before responding. "No, but can we work on your price?"

Now I was confused. Why did he want me to work on my price instead of just getting the better deal elsewhere? I had to ask. "I'm happy that you're here and after hearing about your situation, I would love to work with you, but I'm curious. Why bother when you already have a better deal elsewhere?" Guess who was in the corner now? Instead of me defending my price, he was defending his statement. To make it better, my question in no way made him feel uncomfortable or defensive.

Responding this way does not just support a sale; it supports a conversation. In negotiation, it's not about who is right—it's about who I am as a sales rep and who we are as a company. If we're a good fit for the customer and their specific situation, they'll want to do business with us. And if we're not, they won't, and that is okay, too. What is never okay is to make the customer feel dumb for asking a question, or feel bad about the sales conversation for any reason whatsoever. Earlier in my career, I used to feel defensive when a customer asked for a discount. No doubt they picked up on it and had a negative reaction of their own.

We can't make them feel that they are doing something wrong one minute and then expect them to feel secure with making a decision the next. Instead, we must create an atmosphere that bolsters their confidence, whatever it looks like for that specific customer. Just as I climbed so much better when I felt confident in myself and my situation, customers buy better when they do, too.

Core Principles:

- I must begin with the end in mind.
- I must focus on behaviors.
- I must take action because hope is not enough.
- I must take complete ownership.

SALES PLAN:

Interrupt thought pattern and redirect.

Make them comfortable.

Actively listen.

Let them feel justified.

Set expectations.

Seek out the why.

Discuss money on our terms.

Merge process and expectation.

Build confidence.

TWENTY-ONE

Summit or Bust

I WAS FEELING PRETTY freaking good standing on that small, tree-covered ledge, a mere hundred and forty feet below the summit. Chris ducked under the tree, and we gave each other a high five.

"I can taste the bitter hops of my Founders IPA waiting for me at the car," Chris said as he clipped into the sling.

I dropped down to my butt with my back against the wall and started gathering up gear for the last pitch. A soft wind blew across my face and my sunburned skin. Sitting in the shade of the tree was the first relief we'd had from the sun in hours. As I reached into my pocket, my mind traveled back to where this adventure had begun. While this morning felt like so long ago, the preparation for this day had been in the works for months. I pulled out half of a granola bar and shoved it into my mouth. I was starved and even more so, physically beat. But still one hundred percent motivated to see this through.

As I stood up, I flung the gear over my shoulder and coated my hands heavily in chalk. I gave them a strong slap, and dust filled the air. I let out a howl. "To finishing this!" I jammed my toe on a sloper and pushed off to set my hand in a hole. The last pitch, from what I remembered, was pretty easy. I tiptoed up a few feet and found a hole that took a cam perfectly. I set it, clipped the rope into the carabiner, and kept climbing.

"All aboard the send train!" Chris shouted up.

Shifting my weight from side to side, I waltzed my toes up the rock as my palms pressed against the ripples. I was having fun. The top of the O.R. was starting to slant in a little, and I assumed the position: butt out with weight over the toes and the hands to balance.

A few moments passed when with a jolt I realized I was running this thing way out—the last protection I had placed was far behind me. A surge of anxiety shot through my nervous system, and I stopped in my tracks, panicked. Why was I suddenly certain that I was going to lose traction and fall? I pictured my body splatting against the wall a hundred feet below.

I shut my eyes and exhaled slowly. "You got this, bud," I said, forcing the image out of my mind. I resumed climbing. Through pure mental discipline, I managed to keep myself from doubting my every move. My focus returned to one step and one hand-press at a time. A growth of trees appeared twenty feet above me. I was a hundred feet past my last piece of gear, but I was too exhausted to care. Realizing how close I was, my desire to reach the finish line outweighed any impulse to set pro, which, given the state of the wall, wouldn't have held a fall anyhow. After just a few more steps, I hit the tree line. "Woohoooooo!" The sound crossed high over the valley below before turning around to echo back at me. As I clung to the rock a thousand feet above the valley floor, I was overtaken by emotion. This was real. I had done it—I had led the O.R!

I turned to scramble up, and as I hit the summit, I slung the rope one last time. "Chris! On belay, brother!"

Within a few minutes, Chris came into sight with a smile ear to ear. "Dude, the O.R.! We did it!"

I patted him on the shoulder as I looked out over the edge. What we had just accomplished was more than just a feat; we owned the day. Yup, Chris and I would have this experience to share forever. But more than that—it was an experience I'd shared with this impressive valley and, of course, with the O.R. itself!

"The completed puzzle box"

I firmly believe:

1) we must cultivate core principles for ourselves

2) those principles shape the lens through which we see the world

3) the way we see the world guides our actions

My source of motivation as a sales rep wasn't the trucks I sold—it was the change in the life of the people who purchased them. To be a part of a defining moment in someone's life is a true privilege. With that mentality guiding me, the usual objections, stalls, and off-the-wall expectations transformed from roadblocks into opportunities.

Once we give up the old perspective and start to see things in a different light, the way we view our role also begins to change. And as our thinking changes, so do our actions. This ultimately produces new and better results. Our core principles serve as a powerful guide, and any strategy in alignment with those principles becomes just as powerful.

To recap...

Begin with the end in mind.

In climbing, a body cannot go where the mind has not gone first. I never once stuck my foot on a little chip without my mind first believing I could make the move. But what about experiences where the outcomes are harder to predict? Just as with climbing, we need to see and simulate the steps associated with us getting where we want to be. We have to ensure that every action taken is in alignment with the principles and that every battle we fight leads to winning the war. If we do not, distractions and time-wasting situations will kill our sales record.

Focus on behaviors.

For a repeatable sales strategy that will lead to success, we must focus on our behaviors. The secret to sales is not learning more and more about our products so that we can regurgitate that information to the customers. A customer doesn't buy when they completely and thoroughly understand our product; they buy when they feel understood. The only information that matters is what's going on inside the customer's head. Once we change how we interact with their truth, we see results on the sales report. In other words, we don't earn money by what we tell them, but by the questions we ask them.

Hope without action is not enough.

Sales is not a hope thing; it is not a natural talent thing; it's a will-combined-with-action thing. Any sale that occurs is a direct result of our actions. When a sale does not happen, it's also the result of our actions—or inaction. Reader, allow me to expand on this point. We wouldn't be okay with our income and our livelihood being decided by the astrology section of a newspaper; why should we allow random circumstances, whether favorable or unfavorable, dictate our success? We'll always hope that we get the sale, but without action, hope will get us nowhere. We must take the action necessary to put ourselves in a successful position. There is no such thing as "that is not my job" if the "not my job" thing is what it takes to make the sale.

Take complete ownership.

Accepting responsibility is a game changer, especially when we seek out where we're to blame. It's easy to see our mistakes when the blunders are big (remember when I complimented the customer on his International trucks?). What's more difficult, but far more effective, is looking for the small mistakes in commonplace interactions with potential customers. Seeing and recognizing those faults in our actions allows us to grow enormously; it can create an unstoppable spirit. The more responsibility we take, the more power we give ourselves to influence the outcome. If we deny blame or refuse to accept responsibility, we make the excuse that we truly can't do anything about it. That is disempowering. Owning your actions will do more in creating success than any other behavior or tactic.

AFTERWORD

PARTING SHOT

This is my journey. In a world filled with great ideas, I am fortunate to have found concepts that work not just in the abstract, but in my day-to-day reality. Others have found success by following these very steps, and what an honor it is for me to have been a part of their success. It's gratifying to know that lives and careers have changed by adopting and executing these concepts.

And now to address a few concerns. First off, I already knew my product well when I began my journey of improving my sales technique. While mastering my sales techniques elevated my success, it would have been meaningless without a solid knowledge of the product I sold. Because the trucks I sold were used, not new, the deficiencies or blemishes of each needed to be considered, as well as how the trucks performed. Most importantly, I had to match trucks to the customers' situations and needs.

Secondly, I give quite a few examples of verbiage I've used in sales conversations. These are intended as just that—examples. You'll do best to find your own particular language to improve your sales. And remember, it's not the words we say that are important, but the message the customer hears. Our message and the environment we create combine to change results and influence behavior.

Here's one last disclaimer regarding the sales portion of this book. There are a ton of great sales books out there, and while they differ wildly in approach, there's one message they all share: Don't wing it—have a plan. I couldn't agree more. Purposeful action leads to confidence. As a man I greatly respect once said, "Knowledge leads to confidence, and confidence leads to sales." Amen to that, Jeff!

Regarding the story of my climbs: I am not nor have I ever been a professional climber. This story is not told to boast, or to claim that I've done something that no one else has. In fact, the routes I've climbed have all seen the skid marks and bloodied fingertips of other climbers. I purposefully left out the grades, specifics of difficulty, and locations of routes, because they're not relevant to this story. The feelings I had high up on the O.R. are the exact feelings one could have five feet off the ground.... all of them.

Now forty, I am fortunate to have this journey to look back on. While the drive to accomplish something great was always present, it was never the center of my life. Instead, the center has always been the relationships built, the beautiful places experienced, and the memories created. These alone will remain until my final breath. To that end, I am blessed beyond measure.

A List of My Favorite Business Books

Dianna Booher, *Creating Personal Presence: Look, Talk, Think, and Act Like a Leader*

Bob Burg, *The Art of Persuasion: Winning Without Intimidation*

Shelle Rose Charvet, *Words that Change Minds: The 14 Patterns for Mastering the Language of Influence*

Stephen R. Covey, *The 7 Habits of Highly Effective People: Powerful Lessons in Personal Change*

Joseph Grenny, Kerry Patterson, David Maxfield, Ron McMillan, and Al Switzler, *Influencer: The New Science of Leading Change*

Ben Horowitz, *The Hard Thing about Hard Things: Building a Business When There Are No Easy Answers*

Nick Kolenda, *Methods of Persuasion: How to Use Psychology to Influence Human Behavior*

Patrick Lencioni, *The Four Obsessions of an Extraordinary Executive: A Leadership Fable*

Patrick Lencioni, *The Truth about Employee Engagement: A Fable about Addressing the Three Root Causes of Job Misery*

David Mattson, *The Sandler Rules for Sales Leaders*

Chris McChessney, Sean Covey, and Jim Huling, *The 4 Disciplines of Execution: Revised and Updated: Achieving Your Wildly Important Goals*

Bill Pasmore, *Leading Continuous Change: Navigating Churn in the Real World*

Kerry Patterson, Joseph Grenny, Ron McMillan, and Al Switzler, *Crucial Conversations: Tools for Talking When Stakes are High*

Brian Tracy, *Change Your Thinking, Change Your Life: How to Unlock Your Full Potential for Success and Achievement*

Brian Tracy, *How the Best Leaders Lead: Proven Secrets to Getting the Most Out of Yourself and Others*

Chris Voss, *Never Split the Difference: Negotiating as if Your Life Depended On It*

Made in the USA
Monee, IL
20 May 2022

96798477R00113